A.C. Pinxt. 9th April 1782

COOPER'S IRELAND

First published 2000 by The O'Brien Press Ltd,
20 Victoria Road, Dublin 6, Ireland.
Tel. +353 1 4923333; Fax. +353 1 4922777
E-mail books@obrien.ie
Website www.obrien.ie

ISBN:0-86278-645-2

British Library Cataloguing-in-Publication Data
Harbison, Peter, 1939-
Cooper's Ireland : drawings and notes from an
eighteenth-century gentleman
1.Cooper, Austin 2.Architectural drawing - 18th century -
Ireland
3.Buildings - Ireland - History - 18th century
I.Title II.Cooper, Austin
720.9'415

1 2 3 4 5 6 7 8 9 10
00 01 02 03 04 05 06 07

Castle of Athlumney — Co. Meath

The O'Brien Press receives
assistance from
The Arts Council
An Chomhairle Ealaíon

Layout and design: The O'Brien Press Ltd.
Colour separations: C&A Print Services Ltd.
Printing: Zure, Bilbao, Spain.

Photographs from author's collection: Maiden Tower, front cover; Moret Castle, page 24; Cullahill Castle, 28; Hore Abbey, 30; St Mary's Church, 50; North Abbey, 52; Athassel Abbey, 60; Urlingford Castle, 64; The Gods of the Neale, 72; Naughval Church, 84; Kilkea Castle, 86; Maiden Tower, 96; Cross at Duleek, 116; Burntcourt Castle, 132; Charles Fort, 198; Abbey and Church of Ferns, 204; Boyle Abbey, 218; Kilconnell Cross, 228; Killenure Castle, 240.

Illustrations by Cooper: Front cover: Mallow Castle, Co. Cork; Inside front flap: Banada Abbey, Co. Sligo; Back cover: Charles Fort, Co. Cork; Front end paper: Dunmore Castle, Co. Galway; Back end paper: Trim Castle, Co. Meath.

COOPER'S IRELAND

Drawings and Notes from an Eighteenth-Century Gentleman

PETER HARBISON

National Library of Ireland Mss. 2122 TX (1) and (2)

THE O'BRIEN PRESS
DUBLIN

In association with the National Library of Ireland

CONTENTS

PREFACE AND ACKNOWLEDGEMENTS

More than five years ago, the present holder of the name Austin Cooper, who lives in Northamptonshire, England, kindly agreed to repatriate to Ireland a whole collection of archaeological and historical material, which had descended from his direct ancestor who is the subject of the present volume. This generous gesture was greatly appreciated and facilitated by Dr Pat Donlon, who was Director of the National Library of Ireland at the time. It was her successor, Brendan O Donoghue, who then initiated the creation of the present work and encouraged me to undertake it. To all three I would like to express my gratitude for what I hope will be seen as a valuable contribution to the early history of archaeological studies in Ireland.

Within the National Library, the material was first curated and catalogued by Elizabeth Kirwan. It was her successor as Librarian of Prints and Drawings, Colette O'Daly, who has been of inestimable help in preparing of the Cooper manuscript drawings for publication. To both her and her assistant, Avice-Claire McGovern, I offer my most heartfelt thanks for having made the material accessible to me in an attractive and usable format. Dónall Ó Luanaigh was of great assistance in acquiring the Cooper material for the National Library. In addition, this book would never have seen the light of day without the exceptional skills of Sylvia Lynam in deciphering and making sense of my very difficult manuscript, and producing a beautifully typed text on disk for the publisher.

A number of other people have been a huge help in helping me to obtain accurate and appropriate information for the extended captions to each of Cooper's drawings. I would like to express my grateful thanks to Heather King, Victor Buckley and Chris Corlett of Dúchas; Síobhán Ó Raiffertaigh and Bernie Cunningham of the Royal Irish Academy Library; the late Lena Boylan, Celbridge; Dr Paul Gosling, University College, Galway; Denis Hurley, Castle Mary; Denis Keane, The Neale; Christy Lynch, Limerick; Dr Harman Murtagh, Athlone; Dr Edward McParland, Trinity College, Dublin; Michael Parsons, Portlaoise, and Mr Stanley, Urlingford.

Finally, my thanks to the staff at The O'Brien Press, and in particular Íde ní Laoghaire, Marian Broderick and Ivan O'Brien, for having seen the book successfully through the press.

INTRODUCTION

Austin Cooper (1759–1830)

In Austin Cooper's family, he is known as 'FSA' or 'the Antiquary', not just for descriptive accuracy – for he was indeed a Fellow of the Royal Society of Antiquaries in London – but because he needs to be differentiated from all the other Austin Coopers named after him that are spread over nine generations from his day to the present. The Cooper family's pride in Austin the Antiquary is not misplaced. A high office-holder in the government administration of his time, Cooper was a distinguished gentleman. But it is for his contribution to the nascent study of Ireland's ancient monuments in the late eighteenth century that Austin Cooper is best-remembered. His drawings, and also his diary descriptions of the places he sketched while visiting military establishments and collecting revenue for the government, give the modern reader a fresh insight into the architecture and history of an Ireland long-gone and irreplaceable.

Recent generations of Austin Cooper's descendants have always kept as much as possible of his archaeological material together and have graciously placed it at the disposal of scholars who wished to use it. One of the first historians to realise the potential of the material was Lord Walter FitzGerald of Kilkea Castle, who reproduced a number of drawings of Kildare, Laois and Carlow relevance in the *Journal of the County Kildare Archaeological Society* (1890–1910). But, other than occasional references in F Elrington Ball's six-volume *History of the County of Dublin* (1902–1920) and brief excerpts from Cooper's diaries published in the *Dublin Penny Journal* (1902–1903), it was not until 1942 that Cooper's work was fully explored and the extent of it became known. For, in this year, he was finally given the accolade of having a monograph dedicated to his efforts. This bore the title:

**An
Eighteenth Century
Antiquary**

**The Sketches, Notes and Drawings
of
Austin Cooper (1759–1830)**

The monograph was privately printed by John Falconer of Dublin by direction of Cooper's great-grandson, Albert Damer Cooper, who had left an amount of money in his will to defray the cost of publication of some his ancestor's manuscripts and drawings. What remained, he pointed out, was 'only a small residue of his writings and drawings which has been preserved having been collected by my father at great trouble: for instance, in the case of his diaries, out of 52, we have only 12; all the rest were lost, along with the bulk of his manuscript notes and drawings...'

It is a remarkable tribute to generations of the Cooper family that they were able to keep what they could of manuscripts and diaries together, the material being handed down as it was from one heir to another. For much of this century, the material was kept at Drumnigh House near Portmarnock in north Co. Dublin, but around 1960 it migrated with its then-owner Major Matthew PL Cooper to England. From him, it passed to yet another Austin, Austin EL Cooper, who lives in Nottinghamshire. He had long thought that the material should return to Ireland, where he felt it belonged, and was happy, therefore, to help the National Library of Ireland when it approached him in 1993 with a view to obtaining the Cooper papers for its collection. (It should be said that the material had already been seen and briefly catalogued by the National Library of Ireland the 1950s, and the notes are now preserved there as Mss. 772 and 773.)

When the material was finally repatriated, the National Library divided it up between two departments. Drawings by Cooper and others, as well as engravings of Irish and English interest, went to the Prints and Drawings Department. Those by Cooper – the subject of the present volume – are now preserved there in two albums with the accession number 2122 TX (1) and 2122 TX (2). The literary material in the form of his diaries, together with correspondence, legal documents and so on, are now in the Manuscript Department with the accession number 4841, under which a tentative list of contents can be found, pending its full cataloguing.

Cooper's own drawings, and those of other artists that he collected, provide a very impressive visual record of Ireland's ancient buildings in the last quarter of the eighteenth century. The drawings are a monument to the work of men like Cooper, who felt that it was important to make a record of these structures before they disappeared, which sadly some of them have. For example, the castle at Ticroghan (no.127) in the south-western corner of Co. Meath once looked so imposing that it would not have been out of place in a film set. Yet now, only earthworks remain on the site of this once important and impressive fortification.

Albert Damer Cooper's will stated that 'it would be necessary to get the manuscripts edited prior to publication'. He was fortunate that one of Ireland's best and most discerning amateur antiquarians, the late District Justice Liam Price, agreed to undertake the task that culminated in the 1942 volume mentioned above, which still occasionally makes an appearance in second-hand book catalogues.

In the elegant prose of his introduction, Liam Price tells us most of what we know about the life of Austin Cooper and of the background of his interest in Irish antiquaries. I have no hesitation in referring the reader to this Introduction very warmly indeed – its very existence makes my task easier.

Since then, some further light has been thrown on Cooper's life and family by Richard Austin-Cooper, in his book *Butterhill and Beyond* (1991), privately published at Hurst in Berkshire. Nevertheless, it is now necessary to give a brief summary of Austin Cooper's history, in order to provide a better understanding of the pictures reproduced in the following pages.

The first Coopers of Austin's family came to Ireland from Surrey in southern England in the mid-seventeenth century. His grandfather Samuel, who was born in 1686, settled at Beamore, Co. Meath, not far from Drogheda. Samuel's eldest surviving son, John, was appointed a clerk in the Treasury Office at Dublin Castle in 1742, an office that he held for fifty-one years. The length of his tenure enabled him to get his nephew, Austin the Antiquary, into the service in 1774.

Meanwhile, Uncle John's brother William – the father of our Austin – was appointed registrar with the Diocese of Cashel in 1746, and he settled at Killenure Castle between Cashel and Dundrum in Co. Tipperary. Austin portrayed this castle in what was to be his last on-site drawing among those reproduced in this volume (no.113). He must have sketched it with pleasure and nostalgia, for it was there that he was born in February 1759, and there that he spent the first fifteen years of his life, with interruptions for early schooling in Cashel. Perhaps it seems harsh to us today that he was not yet sixteen when he was sent off to join the Treasury Office under the tutelage of Uncle John, but for company he had a kinsman, Joseph Cooper Walker, with whom he formed a long-lasting friendship. Austin, Joseph and the latter's brother, Samuel, all shared an interest in what must have been the 'in-thing' at the time, namely antiquities.

Not long after Cooper entered the service, the office of the Teller of the Exchequer was filled by one Colonel William Burton, who was to take the name Conyngham when he took over Slane Castle in Co. Meath in 1781. In 1779, Burton founded the Hibernian Antiquarian Society, a very select group of only seven people. The Society's purpose was to record ancient Irish architecture for posterity, and to gather or commission drawings that could then be engraved in one or more volumes to show off the beauties and glories of Ireland's ancient monuments. Through bickering among its members, the Society collapsed after only four years, without having achieved its aim. The only member to really benefit from the scheme was Edward Ledwich. Ledwich used much of the material that Burton had collected to illustrate Grose's *Antiquities of Ireland,* which he edited after the death of a man Cooper described as 'my friend Capt. Grose', in the diary entry for 16 May 1791.

Liam Price is surely right to suggest that it was Burton's influence that encouraged Cooper to use his talents as a draughtsman in support of the Society's aims, though Cooper was probably too young at the time to be considered for membership. It is certainly interesting to note that Cooper's earliest dated drawing here – St Mary's in Drogheda (no.81) – was executed on Christmas Day, 1778, just two months before Burton established the

Antiquarian Society. In other words, Cooper, though not yet twenty, was already drawn to ancient monuments, and was aware that this was also a particular interest of the man who was his boss, William Burton.

Therefore it is likely that Cooper's enthusiasm in drawing ancient monuments was of strategic advantage to him, for he was appointed Paymaster to the Pensioners on the Civil and Military Establishments when only in his early thirties, and thus promoted to undertake responsible tasks involving considerable amounts of money. In his diary for 28 March 1791, he records departing from Dublin on a tour 'to bring up the Collector's Balance' and he noted a number of instances where he settled with the Collector, not to mention 'reckoning silver' in Limerick on Sunday, 3 March, of the same year. This would suggest that he was also involved in collecting revenue. To carry out such functions, he needed an escort of guards, which he portrays in the drawing of Cloghleagh Castle, Co. Cork (no.68). Travelling around the country in such style gave him the opportunity to stop occasionally and indulge his talents for sketching the plentiful ruins. Understandably, most of his drawings are of monuments visible from the main roads on which he was travelling.

The dates on the drawings show that in 1781, when he was only twenty-two, and long before he was promoted, he had already undertaken an extended tour of Munster, and the contents of this first album of drawings are dated up until 1785. The contents of the second volume cover spasmodic activity over the following nine years, and we can see from it that his sphere of activity was mainly in the southern half of the country. In addition, visits to his brother in Roscrea must have often brought him back to his native county. His forays to counties Meath and Louth may have been personal expeditions undertaken from the old family homestead at Beamore, with which he kept up contact, as the diaries reveal. It is only on rare occasions that he recorded items in Connacht and Ulster, and there his obvious interest in Round Towers played a role in his selection of subject. This can be seen in his choice of the Clones and Antrim towers (nos.79 and 103) – the latter of which he sketched on a rare trip to the north in June 1791, when he also visited the Giant's Causeway in Co. Antrim.

As mentioned above, Cooper's last surviving on-site drawing was dated 1793 – the same year that he succeeded his Uncle John as Chief Clerk of the Treasury. The onerous duties which he took on with his new position probably kept him more at home, and left him with much less time – if any – to gallivant around the country, although he sated his antiquarian appetite late in 1794 by copying drawings into his second album. Though the *Gentleman's Almanack* of 1799 listed him as Military Clerk to the Commissioners of the Exchequer, which may still have given him some opportunity for travelling, the important appointment as Deputy Constable of Dublin Castle in 1796 must have confined him largely to the capital. He held this post until his death in 1830, and the badge of his office – a black axe – is still preserved as an heirloom in the family.

In spite of his official duties, Cooper had time to act as land agent for some members of the aristocracy, which, according to Liam Price, included Lord Leitrim, Lord Conyngham and Sir Francis Nathaniel Burton. He was also an agent for the State Lottery, in which he is said to have won a prize of £20,000. With money like that, it was no wonder that he could buy the famous Gandon mansion at Abbeyville near Kinsealy, into which he moved in 1815. He also bought lands at nearby Drumnigh, and he also had property at Drumhallagh in Donegal, but the later years of his life he seems to have spent mainly in his Dublin townhouse at 4 Merrion Square North. It was there that he died on 30 August 1830, having never recovered fully from breaking his leg in a carriage accident as he drove from Abbeyville to Dublin the previous year. He is buried in the family vault in the old ruined church near the Kinsealy–Portmarnock road.

The year after his death, Cooper's extensive library was sold off at auction, of which the National Library holds a catalogue. It was at this auction that George Petrie, an antiquary of a younger generation, who knew Austin Cooper, bought for the Royal Irish Academy the autograph copy of the *Annals of the Four Masters,* which John O'Donovan used for his masterly seven-volume printed edition in the 1850s. Liam Price states that Petrie also bought some of the drawings from Cooper's library, but it is unknown to which ones he was referring, or what became of them.

We can be certain that the surviving material is only a fraction of what there once was. Cooper obviously kept a daily diary for about 50 years, but only the years 1782, 1784, 1791, 1795–96, 1803–1804, 1808, 1811–12, 1815 and 1830 survive. They give details of his private life, mainly the comings and goings of members of his family, including his cousins Samuel and Joseph Cooper Walker, and stories of those with whom he sat down to dinner. They included the aristocracy, but also people such as James Gandon, the architect of the Kinsealy mansion that was later to be his.

Further to the diaries, there are a number of notebooks arranged by counties or places, most of which – though not all – correspond to the areas covered by the drawings. The individual volumes are of Co. Dublin; parts of South Co. Kildare and adjoining districts; Cashel; the route from Dublin to Killaloe; parts of counties Limerick and Waterford; south Tipperary; Tuam, Co Galway; and Drogheda, Co Meath. There is also a description of

Kilmacduagh in Co. Galway. The order of the entries is not always chronological, suggesting to Liam Price – doubtless correctly – that they represent field notes subsequently worked up into album form. It is the contents of these notebooks together with interesting snippets from the diary (excluding those already published in the *Dublin Penny Journal* of 1902–1903) that form the main part of the text of the Liam Price volume on Austin Cooper. Because the texts are printed there almost in their entirety, it is unnecessary to repeat them here, and only those sections that are of value in illustrating the drawings are quoted in the captions to the illustrations in this volume.

Liam Price refers to drawings by Austin Cooper, particularly a set showing buildings of Co. Dublin, that were shown to Sir William Wilde by J Huband Smith around the middle of the nineteenth century, but their present whereabouts – if they survive at all – remains a mystery. A further seven drawings re-surfaced recently in Messrs Mealy's auction in Castlecomer, Co. Kilkenny, in early December 1999. These had been sold to a private collector in the early 1960s, and have recently been published by Conleth Manning in *The Journal of Irish Archaeology* Vol. 7, 1999, as listed in the Appendix on p.282. The National Library has now acquired two of them. These seven may well have belonged to another album similar to the two published here, and their existence provides hope that there may be others lurking in private collections, which may yet see the light of day. It is a pleasant thought that this volume might help any other drawings to be recognised for what they are, and encourage their owners to bring them out of their hiding places.

The drawings reproduced here all come from Mss 2122 TX (1) and (2) in the National Library of Ireland. The originals are all black-and-white pen and wash illustrations of various sizes, always on a right-hand page in the albums and probably all using Whatman paper with crown and fleurs-de-lis watermarks. Most are in a rectangular format but this is occasionally varied by the use of round or oval frames. The majority of Cooper's drawings reproduced here were sketched in the field while Cooper was touring around the country sometimes two or three times a year, and later carefully re-worked into a clean copy on the album page.

The date of the originals he normally gives on the bottom left accompanied by his monogram AC and the word *delint,* short for *delineavit,* meaning 'he drew'. Correspondingly on bottom right is the word *pinxt* for *pinxit,* meaning 'he painted', referring to the actual picture reproduced here, giving a date, though sometimes without the year being given. Both volumes follow the rough chronological order in which the *originals* were executed – but this is not necessarily the order in which they were painted in the album. This peculiarity we can see in the very first illustrations where no.3 (the heads of the two effigies from Great Connell and Fertagh respectively) was painted in September 1785, while the picture of Kildare Round Tower on the following page was painted on November 19, 1784. That this happens on a number of occasions, particularly between nos.27 and 32, suggests that Cooper may have left a number of pages blank to fill in later. The anomaly of St Mary's in Drogheda (no.81) being given a painting date of 1775 may, however, suggest a lapse of Cooper's part, as the original was painted in 1778 and none of the previous painted illustrations is earlier than 1781.

It was mainly his own originals that Cooper copied into the first album, as we can see from the signature *AC delin* on the bottom left corner. But there are a few instances when he copied drawings by others artists. In nos.28–30, William and Ralph Ouseley – two brothers of a distinguished Galway family – provided the originals, those by William painted when he was only nineteen years of age. Another contributor was William Leeson, probably from Loughrea, Co. Galway, who, as Dr Edward McParland kindly informs me, was the architect of Kilboy and Traverston in Co. Tipperary as well as Clonbrock, Prior Park and Pallas in Co. Galway. If we can judge by Cooper's copies, Leeson's sense of perspective shown in the views of Abbeyknockmoy, Co. Galway (no.72 and 73) is rather peculiar. This strong Galway connection in the first volume is not easy to explain, as neither Ouseley nor Leeson seem to find mention in Cooper's surviving diaries of the period.

But one name that does come up in the diaries is that of 'Sam' – probably the Samuel Cooper Walker who was a cousin of Cooper's. Sam was a very competent artist as is demonstrated by his minutely detailed drawing of Cashel crozier in the Cooper collection, which was published recently by Monica Nevin in the *Journal of the Royal Society of Antiquaries* (1995). Cooper's diaries indicate that Sam and Cooper often dined together, and Cooper noted with concern whenever Sam was unwell. As suggested by the two illustrations of the Maiden's Tower at Mornington (no.41) – one by Cooper and the other by Walker, but both done on the same day – the two obviously went on sketching trips together, probably from the Cooper property at Beamore near Drogheda. Walker's original 1783 drawings of Duleek monuments, copied a month later by Cooper (nos.50–52), may have been done from the same base, while his representation of Tyrrel's Mills at Celbridge (no.90) may have been part of an expedition from another Cooper family home, the Barn, near Leixlip.

On pp.699–700 of Vol. VII of John Bowyer Nichols' *Illustrations of the Literary History of the Eighteenth Century* (London, 1848) records that, in 1787, Joseph Cooper

Walker sent off a list of drawings in the possession of Austin Cooper to Richard Gough in London. They were intended for Gough's new edition of Camden's *Britannia*. Gough replied that 'if a folio plate could be comprised of eighteen round towers from Mr Cooper's drawings I would gladly engrave it'. Sadly, despite a thorough search by Dr Niamh Whitfield for Round Tower drawings among Gough's publications in the library of the Society of Antiquaries in London, nothing further to this correspondence has turned up. It would appear that Gough never used Cooper's material after all. However, the Ouseley Commonplace Scrapbook, Ms 5905 (pp.214–215) in the National Library of Ireland, does contain a series of Round Tower drawings from 1788 – comprising eighteen frames with seventeen towers – which may be a copy of what Walker offered Gough.

Two other artists whose works were copied by Cooper in the first volume deserve to be mentioned here. The first is Anthony Chearnley, whose 1744 drawings of his own house at Burntcourt, Co. Tipperary (nos.58–59), were both copied by Cooper into the first volume, and whose Ardfinnan drawing of the same year was copied into the second volume (no.91). Along with the 1755 Tarrant drawing of the Market Cross in Kilkenny, this is by far the oldest material copied into the album, the originals being already forty years in existence before Cooper reproduced them. The three Chearnley pictures were reproduced in Grose's *Antiquities,* where they are stated to have been in the collection of William Burton (later Conyngham), and it must have been he who allowed Cooper to copy the drawings.

The second of those other artists whose works Cooper copied in the first volume was JJ Barralet. It was presumably on Conyngham's instructions that he went to Wexford in 1780 to record ancient monuments in the county, accompanied by Gabriel Beranger, who had been commissioned to do the same for Connacht a year previously. On that tour, Beranger was accompanied by Italian stage designer Angelo Maria Bigari, who also made a number of drawings in the province. The products of their pens and watercolours became part of Conyngham's collection – and therefore it is again through Conyngham's goodwill that Cooper was able to copy so much of their material into his second volume. Most of the other drawings in the second volume that Cooper copied from other artists' originals must also have come from Conyngham. The fact that the same originals were also copied by other artists, including Beranger, demonstrates just how happy Conyngham must have been to share his enthusiasm about these ancient monuments with his contemporaries. Artists whose work Cooper copied into his second album include well-known names, such as Colonel Charles Vallancey (Kinsale, Ardmore and Clarecastle), himself a member of the Hibernian Antiquarian Society, the painters Thomas Sautelle Roberts (Dunmoe, no.129) and Jonathan Fisher (Slane, no.130). Also included are others who worked for Conyngham but about whom very little is known – Mr Monk (Fore, no.109), PS Reilly (Taghadoe, no.120), whose work was engraved for Grose's *Antiquities,* the Reverend Mr Seymour (Garran Castle, no.131) and Thomas Ashworth (Clonard, no.126 and Ticroghan, no.127).

The availability of these original drawings in the Conyngham collection from 1779 onwards must have shown Cooper which monuments he should look out for in his travels. Liam Price notes the fact that Cooper's views of monuments were inevitably taken from a different angle to those shown in the Conyngham collection of drawings as engraved in Grose's *Antiquities*. This suggests that Cooper must have studied the Conyngham collection carefully before setting out on his journeys, and deliberately determined to draw the majority of pictures himself, but from a different angle. Yet, curiously, the traffic seems all to have been one way; Grose's *Antiquities*, published in two volumes in the 1790s, was heavily dependant on originals in the Conyngham collection for its illustrations, but does not use any Cooper drawings, possibly because there were none in the Conyngham collection. However, its editor, Edward Ledwich, did have a Cooper drawing of Athassel (no.23) engraved for his own *Antiquities of Ireland* (1791).

There are two unique features of the second album – 2122 TX (2) – which one would not expect in an artist's own book of drawings. The first of these is that other artists have put their *own* drawings into the album, including William Ouseley, whom we have already met. Another artist included in the book – and very much a 'dark horse' – is one JJ Russell, probably a Limerick artist, whose picture of Castletroy Castle in the grounds of the new University of Limerick reveals a hidden talent.

The second even more unexpected feature is that a considerable number of drawings were copied into Cooper's album by various members of his extended family. Originals by Beranger, Bigari, Vallancey, the architect Thomas Ivory, the painters Fisher and Foster, and the Reverends Seymour and Hume, doubtless artists all represented in the Conyngham collection at the time, were copied into Cooper's album by his relations in 1794. One of these was Sarah, Cooper's wife and the mother of his eight children, whom he had married in 1786 and who contributes one drawing of a Bigari original showing Inishmurray. Another Cooper kinsman, JS Cooper, is also known to have been involved in the copying process. But the person who did most copying into the second volume was Joseph Turner, occasionally given as the 'Rev. Jos. Turner'. He is probably the man Cooper mentions in his diaries of the 1780s as coming to dine occasionally, and was probably the brother of

Cooper's wife Sarah, whose maiden name was Turner. He is probably also the Joseph Turner who is in the records of the Representative Church Body as having been rector of Slane around 1800 – probably a living that was in the gift of Conyngham – and who was rector of Raddanstown, Co. Meath when he died in 1835. These family copies by JS Cooper, Sarah Cooper and Jos Turner are not of particularly high quality, and are not reproduced here but are listed on p.281.

Liam Price's book – *An Eighteenth Century Antiquary,* referred to above – included a judicious selection of all of these various categories: Cooper's copies of his own drawings and those of other artists, originals by other artists, and family members' copies of other artists' work. In addition, it also includes ground plans of monuments and good sketches by other artists, which are among material on separate sheets that formed part of the Cooper collection. But, as Liam Price explained in his

Introduction to the 1942 work, the financial constraints of those days prevented inclusion of all the Austin Cooper drawings. It was doubtless this fact, and the comparative rarity of copies of the Price volume, that inspired Brendan O Donoghue, Director of the National Library of Ireland, actively to encourage the writing of this book, as a fitting tribute to the man who helped preserve visual records of our archaeological and architectural heritage.

Together with the Beranger watercolours and the engravings in Grose's *Antiquities,* the Cooper drawings contained herein form the greatest compendium of visual records of Ireland's historic monuments as they were in the late eighteenth century. As such, they form a foundation stone for the emergence of archaeology in Ireland, and provide an important documentary source for study. In addition to the artistic merit of the two albums, their very existence is reason and incentive enough to publish, in full, works that now form part of the nation's heritage.

CELBRIDGE CHURCH, Co. KILDARE

Austin Cooper's interest in Co. Kildare, where he sketched a number of historical monuments including the church at Celbridge reproduced opposite, was probably inspired by the fact that he had relatives at Barn Hill, near the interestingly named Wonderful Barn close to Leixlip. As Lena Boylan, the recently deceased doyenne of Celbridge history, pointed out, Cooper even had a lease interest in some land nearby at Parsonstown at one stage in his career.

It was presumably during a visit to Barn Hill that he sketched this church in the Tea Lane graveyard in Celbridge. This he did from over the wall, probably because from within the churchyard he was unable to position himself far enough back to include the whole structure.

The crenellated tower may be a remnant of an earlier church on the site, and is the only part of the building to have survived reasonably (though not entirely) intact. Its steeple was demolished only three years after Cooper had drawn it, and much of the early eighteenth-century nave with its simple, round-headed, traceried windows has disappeared,

with the exception of the ruined east gable. One small part near the tower, however, has been transformed into the vault of the Maunsell family, of nearby Oakley Park.

The more famous mausoleum here is the Death House, the burial place of Speaker Conolly (1662–1729), who built the great Palladian mansion at Castletown, about half a mile away. The Death House was originally a mortuary chapel built on to the north side of the church, and accessible from it through a doorway now blocked up. Today it is a locked and lightless room, containing fine effigies of the Speaker and his wife, which were carved in the 1730s by Thomas Carter of London.

The churchyard was also the burial place of the family of Henry Grattan (though not of the great parliamentarian himself, who lies interred in Westminster Abbey), and also of the Dongans, one of whose number was Governor of New York between 1683 and 1688.

Lady Louisa Conolly replaced the church when she built a new one inside the gates of Castletown in 1806.

AC delin. 11 March 1781 —

A N.W. View of **Celbridge** Church, Co. Kildare

GREAT CONNELL ABBEY, Co. KILDARE

The Abbey of Great-Connell (Coy. Kildare) is so decayed, that scarcely any descriptive Acct. can be given of it's remaining Ruins. One part, which I suppose to be both Nave & Choir, but between which no distinct separation can be made, measures about 200 ft. long & 25 ft. broad, in part whereof are two entire Gothic Windows, the only ones which have resisted the Ravages of Time &c. There are very extensive ruins adjoining in which are some Pillars &c. with curious Capitals.

These are the opening sentences of Austin Cooper's description of a tour of Munster, which he started on 14 May 1781. Great Connell Abbey – only about two miles from Newbridge – was probably the first historical monument he visited on the trip and certainly the first one he drew.

What his drawing shows are the remains of the abbey as it was in his day, with the east gable of the church on the extreme left, and parts of the north and south walls, with nave arcades and probably fragments of the claustral buildings, further to the right. Today, only the east gable remains, gapped for a no-longer existing window, much as Cooper showed it. The other masonry that Cooper illustrates was removed more than a century ago. It provided stones for the construction of a barracks in Newbridge, and for the rebuilding of a private residence at nearby Connellmore. Unfortunately, not a trace can be found of those 'curious capitals' that Cooper mentioned in his account.

The neglected gable is a sad remnant of a once important priory founded for the Augustinian Canons around 1202 by Meiler FitzHenry, a bastard son of King Henry I of England. A decree of 1476 stated that the priory had been impoverished because the previous abbot had given grants to the 'Irishry' – perhaps a gesture of reconciliation to make up for the fact that the Irish were excluded from joining the English-dominated monastery during much of the fourteenth century.

Among the fine effigies removed from Great Connell to St Brigid's Cathedral in Kildare town are those of two priors, one of which is illustrated overleaf (no.3). The other effigy is of Walter Wellesley, who fought hard to keep the monastery open at the start of the Reformation, and it is the finest of its kind surviving from the end of the medieval period in Ireland. When Great Connell was finally suppressed a year after Wellesley's death in 1539, it was described as having a belfry and a chapel of the Blessed Virgin.

Other possessions listed at the time of its closure – 1260 acres of land, a mill and five castles – show that it was a rich foundation. We know it also to have been, historically, a centre of considerable learning because, in 1237, its scriptorium produced a handsome manuscript of the *Ecclesiastica Historica* by Eusebius, which is now preserved in the library of Hereford Cathedral.

AB delin.14. May 1781.   Pinx.7th July.

A W: View of the Abbey of **Great Connel** Co. Kildare

OLD TOMBS AT GREAT CONNELL, Co. KILDARE (A), AND FERTAGH, Co. KILKENNY (B)

Cooper temporarily abandons his usual square format here order to concentrate on the head-dresses of two medieval effigies, as he himself admits in the right-hand caption. The episcopal effigy on the left, which he drew at the Abbey of Great Connell (see no.2) in Co. Kildare on 14 May 1781, he described briefly in his diary for that day as follows:

> Buried among the ruins is the Tomb of a Bp. (I suppose Wellesley) in relievo, in his Robes, with a Canopy over his head. It is broke across at the Neck & the lower part is scarcely to be seen.

He is mistaken in supposing this to be the effigy of Wellesley, which is still complete, and was removed to St Brigid's Cathedral, Kildare, in 1971. This effigy, whose identity has yet to be satisfactorily established, was also removed to Kildare Cathedral, where it is displayed near the western end of the nave. In his book *Irish Medieval Figure Sculpture*, John Hunt dated it to the early fourteenth century. In addition to the break across the neck that Cooper describes, it had a further accident in 1969 when a tree fell across it.

It was at the start of his tour of Munster that Cooper stopped at Great Connell. Just two days later he made a

further stop to draw the second of this pair of effigy-heads at Fertagh, or Grangefertagh, in Co. Kilkenny. This effigy is preserved in a church at the foot of a Round Tower, which stands out conspicuously on the north side of the Dublin–Cork road a few miles from Johnstown in Co. Kilkenny.

Here, Cooper focuses his attention on the head of a lady, part of a double effigy on top of a box tomb, which was erected to the memory of John MacGillapatrick, lord of Ossory, and his son Brian, during the first half of the sixteenth century. Since the accompanying inscription states that it was Brian's mother who erected the tomb, she was also presumably John's wife. The barbe, or veil, that falls from the twin points of her head-dress, and covers her chin, indicates that she was a widow when the effigy was carved. The bright, horizontal strip across the upper part of the picture is the pillow upon which her head rests. A product of the famous stonemason workshop of the O'Tunney family, the effigy is sadly not as 'nearly perfect' as it was when Cooper drew it nearly 220 years ago.

Cooper's cousin, Joseph C. Walker, used this Cooper drawing in his *Historical Essay on the Dress of the Ancient and Modern Irish*, published in London in 1788.

Ab. delin. 24ᵗʰ May 1785.

Dinᵈ. 21ᵗ Septᵇ. 1785.

W. delin. 15ᵗʰ May 1785.

The Remains of an Old Tomb in the Abbey of **Great Connel** *᷉ Coᵗʸ Kildare ᷉ Supposed to be that of Bishop* **Wellesley** *᷉*

See Harris's Bps. p. 309 ᷉

Part of an Old Tomb in the **Church** *of* **Fertagh** *᷉ Coᵗʸ Kilkenny ᷉*

N.B: This Figure & that of a Man on her right hand remain nearly perfect ᷉ This part was copied only to shew the Head-dress ᷉

ROUND TOWER, Kildare

Austin Cooper was no slouch, for on the same day that he did the drawings of Great Connell (nos.2 and 3), he had time to stop at Kildare and make a sketch of the Round Tower. This, together with some details of the doorway, he copied into his album some three and a half years later. In his diary, he recorded that:

> …the round Tower here is 18 yards in Circumfe. – inside diam. 5 ft. 4 in. – the Wall 3 ft. 6 in. The door is from the ground, 5 ft. 2 in. high and 1 ft. 9 in. broad, faces nearly S. and has it's sides & arch Work beautifully wrought with fine red Free Stone – the Inside is divided into Stories by five rings of projecting Stones (one a little below the door) with a window in each, & four large ones in the upper story; the Top is cap'd, with a hole thro' it, & at the same time embattled.

Standing at a height of more than 100ft, the tower is situated to the west of the thirteenth-century cathedral in the centre of Kildare town, and, during the tourist season, can be climbed to the top. Cooper's view is fairly accurate except for the doorway, which does not have a keyhole shape and is symmetrically beneath the tangent gable above it. This doorway, which Cooper forgot to note was about 15ft above ground, is decorated on the innermost arch with a flower design in a lozenge on the soffit. Cooper also gives a rather stylised version of the almost tree-like pattern on the capital preserved on the south side. This decoration clearly shows that the doorway fits into the Romanesque style of the second half of the twelfth century.

The bottom nine layers of the tower are of granite, while the layers above them are of limestone. Previous observers believed that the granite part belonged to an earlier tower, and the limestone to a subsequent re-building. However, because coins of no earlier than the 1140s were found in the mortar bedding of the tower, we can safely assume the whole tower is of the same period as the Romanesque decoration of the doorway, which places it comparatively late in the Irish Round Tower series. However, the battlements that Cooper mentioned above were added earlier in the eighteenth century.

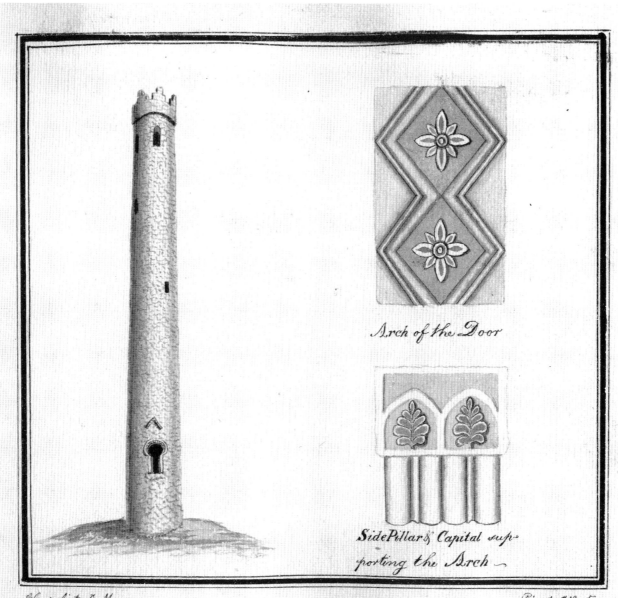

Arch of the Door

SidePillar & Capital sup-
porting the Arch

A:C delint 14th May 1781

Pinxt 19th Novr 1784

Tower at Kildare

MORET CASTLE, Co. Laois

To the left of the road from Monasterevin to Portlaoise, a traveller will see parts of the gables of a ruined building. This is Moret Castle which, as we can see from Cooper's illustration, was in a much better state of preservation when he sketched it on 15 May 1781. In his diary, Cooper records that:

> It does not seem to be very ancient, as the work is quite fresh, & altogether it has a modern Appearance. The inside is quite black, as if it had been burned & without any Stairs. From some little Banks &c remaining, I imagine it to have been surrounded by a Fosse &c. The Wall is 4 ft. 8 ins. It is said to have been built by the FitzGeralds.

Only eleven years later, Lieutenant Daniel Grose visited the castle. His drawing of it – taken from the north-west – was published in Vol. II of *The Antiquities of Ireland,* a publication that was started by his uncle, Francis Grose, and edited by Edward Ledwich after Francis's death. Daniel described the castle as 'one of those castellated houses which, in rude and perturbed times, were necessary for security from danger' and noted that it had 'a stack of chimnies in each side wall and gable end.' Two of these can be seen in Cooper's drawing, and the diamond-shaped cross-section of each chimney would suggest a building date of not earlier than the second half of the sixteenth century.

For centuries, the land on which the castle stands had been in the hands of the FitzGerald earls of Kildare, whose family possessions, including 'the castles and manors of Ley and Morette', were forfeited to the crown after 'Silken' Thomas FitzGerald's unsuccessful rebellion in 1534. It is possible that this forfeited castle was a previous building on the site of the present ruins. Indeed, one Gerald FitzGerald had acquired the lease of a castle on the site in 1585, but it was burned down by an O'More in revenge for the death of one Fergus O'Kelly of Timogue, allegedly at the hands of the same Gerald FitzGerald.

While the rounded bartizans at the corner – of which two survive – give the current castle a somewhat defensive appearance, the large windows show that this was a castellated house, which was built more as a home than a fortification. The walls between the two surviving gables fell more than a century ago according to Lord Walter FitzGerald, who provided us with a brief history of the castle in the 1904 issue of the *Journal of the County Kildare Archaeological Society*, where he reproduced this drawing by Austin Cooper.

J.C. delin.t 15.th May 1791   Pinx.t 8.th July

An E: View of Moret Castle, Queen's Co.

CHURCH OF CASTLE-DURROW, CO. LAOIS

This church stood in the village of Durrow in what is now Co. Laois, only a few paces from Cooper's route from Dublin to Cork. In the eighteenth century, this part of Laois – or the Queen's County as it was then known – was annexed by the neighbouring Co. Kilkenny, so that the Butlers could more easily get their hands on the Fitzpatrick lords of the locality. The land was only returned to Co. Laois around 1836–37.

'The church is very plain' is Cooper's apt comment. It was a low, broad, rectangular structure with a double door in the gable, topped by a belfry, and with two round-headed windows on one of the long sides. The presence of a buttress between the windows would suggest a building unstable enough to need support. However, the church was barely two centuries old when Cooper sketched it on 16 May 1781, the day after sketching Moret Castle (no.5). It is quite likely that Cooper was on a refreshment stop in the village barracks en route from Moret Castle when he made this drawing.

Today not a trace of the old church can be seen, but most likely it stood on the site of the present Protestant church (built 1793), beside the attractive village green.

'The town of Durrow', Cooper wrote, 'is small, but neat, with a spacious area in the center, wherein are some good houses, & likewise a small Market-house with a square Cupola & Clock, dated 1753.' But Cooper's main interest lay in the 'fine seat' of Lord Ashbrook up the hill, at the end of the avenue, beside the church. He continues:

> The front of this house is of limestone, with four Doric Pilasters supporting a suitable cornice, over each of which are Pedestals with urns & within them a Hip roof with 5 dormant windows, & a number of Chimnies. Between each Pilaster there are three Windows, the lower range whereof are ornamented with circular & angular pediments alternately. The Door-case consists of two Doric pilasters with a proper cornice, supporting two Urns; between the Tryliphs 1716, which date is likewise on the leaden Spouts. The whole laid out in an old Stile, very little altered, owing to the Non-residence of his Lordship.

The Ashbrooks, whose family name was Flower, finally sold the estate in 1922. The house then served as a convent school before being sold recently to a new owner, who is hoping to restore the original attractive exterior to the house, and then convert it into a hotel.

A.C: delin.t 16.th May 1781

Pinxt. 6.th Sep.t

A N.W: View of the Church of **Castle-Durrow** Co.y Kilkenny

CULLAHILL CASTLE, Co. Laois

After sketching the church at Durrow (no.6), Cooper immediately went his way, and four miles along the Cork road, he encountered the castle of Cullahill – or 'Cullyhill', as he called it. There, he would appear to have met a well-dressed local guide, who we can see gesturing in the bottom left of Cooper's drawing (opposite). Pointing out that the 'stairs at present (strait flights) lead to but two stories', Cooper mentions this cicerone with some affection:

> A Man there, (who knew the impossibility of my getting up farther, to determine the Truth of his Narrative,) told me very plausibly, that his Father was once on the Top & found an Inscription on one of the stones, which, tho' a good Scholar, he could not read.

Cooper described the castle as:

> … a strong Building; three sides whereof is surrounded with a strong wall & towers, between wch. & the Case.

[Castle] is a narrow passage with Spike holes for defence. In the upper parts are Gangways for the same purpose, the wall being 12 ft. thick. The north side of this Case. Is fallen down; from whence was the Communication to the adjoining Yard & Offices, surrounded with a strong Wall & Ditch. A Well in the Yard.

Still presenting a striking feature on the Dublin–Cork road, the castle has luckily suffered little change in the last 200 years, though it must be said that trees now prevent as good a view of the castle as Cooper got from his vantage point.

The pile of rubble on the left – looking like a pyramid – doubtless comes from that part of the castle which had collapsed. But the surrounding wall, with its attractive corner turrets, gives us an excellent idea of just what those bawns looked like in the medieval period, when they protected the people within the castle, and the livestock without.

AC.delin.16.May 1781.   Sine.23.Nov.1784.

Castle of **Cullyhill** *Queen's Co.*

HORE ABBEY, CASHEL, Co. TIPPERARY

By 17 May 1781, Cooper had reached Cashel, and there he stayed for a few days. On 19 May, he records visiting Hore Abbey, which stands at the foot of St Patrick's Rock.

Hore Abbey had been founded in 1272 at the instigation of the Archbishop of Cashel, David McCarville, and was the last Cistercian house to open in Ireland before the Reformation. It is unique among Irish Cistercian monasteries in having the cloister located to the north of the church, but otherwise it shows little change from its twelfth-century predecessors, particularly in the arrangement of two chapels in the east wall of each transept. In his diary, Cooper made a plan of the Abbey, explaining – through the addition of letters – the various parts of the building, and giving detailed measurements and heights, though he did find difficulty in giving names to some sections of the Cistercian complex.

Cooper's interestingly shaded 'view', as he calls it, differs very little from the real thing that we can see today. He chooses to concentrate on the building itself, and does not include the dramatic backdrop of the Rock of Cashel, which can be seen when looking at the building from a slightly different angle.

Although only two of the five nave arcades are blocked today, four out of the five are blocked in Cooper's sketch. This is a reminder that, after the monastery was dissolved in 1540, the buildings were converted into domestic housing, after the Abbey and its lands had passed into the possession of James Butler, earl of Ormond. That, too, is a part of the history of this Cistercian house, which should not be forgotten.

A.C. delin.t 16.th May 1781.

Print.d 10.th July

A S: view of Hore-Abbey near Cashell Co.y Tipperary.

HORE ABBEY, CASHEL, Co. TIPPERARY

One of the things that caught Cooper's eye when he visited Hore Abbey on 19 May 1781 was the vaulting beneath the crossing tower. The description given in his diary runs as follows:

> The steeple is large, abt 20 feet square withinside & supported by two fine Arches abt. 30 ft high – the inside is supported by a variety of Ogives from each angle, some meeting in an octagon in the center, & others at the key stones of the vault. The upper part is entirely open ....

On this day, Cooper chose to concentrate on the ogives meeting at the centre in an octagon – making them look somewhat like the mast-top rigging of a medieval sailing craft.

However, instead of showing the three nave windows in the blank arched space in the centre of the sketch, Cooper omits them, leaving the vaulting without a context, and thus making this drawing almost an exercise in abstract art.

The tower and the vaulting were, in fact, a fifteenth-century addition to the thirteenth-century monastery building and, as Roger Stalley points out, they are a typical example of the Ormond architecture of the time. But Cooper had an eye for small, interesting sculptural details as well as the overall effect, and, in his diary, he noted down two mason's marks, a Butler shield shown as if hanging on the wall – and what looks like an IHS monogram on the arches of the tower.

A.C. delin.^t 18.th May 1781.   Pinx.^t 25.th Aug.^t

Inside of the Arch supporting the Steeple of

Hore-Abbey *near* **Cashell**

MUNGRET ABBEY, Co. LIMERICK

When Austin Cooper made this drawing of what he called the 'Abbey of Mungret' in 1781, the tower on the right probably stood out as the tallest building in the locality. Nowadays, it is dwarfed by the large cement works, half a mile away, which at least has the advantage of making the church easy to find from a distance.

This church is one of a group of three on an ancient monastic site – one of the churches has a classic Irish lintel doorway, probably built before the twelfth century. The site upon which the churches stand was founded by a deacon named Nessan, who died in 551. Records show that one of the subsequent abbots of the monastery – possibly in the seventh century – was regarded as something of a human computer, as he was consulted by eminent authorities on the besetting problem of when the feast of Easter should be celebrated.

Located not far from the Shannon estuary, and being too close to the city of Limerick for its own safety, the monastery later found itself subject to raids from both Norse and Irish. Around the twelfth century the monastery began to decline on foot of the monastic reform sweeping Ireland, helped along by Gilbert, the Bishop of Limerick, among others.

The church (now locked) in the drawing is located in a stony churchyard about a hundred yards along a small road off the main thoroughfare. Since it was built after the decline of the monastery, it is more correctly described as a parish church, according to Canon Michael Moloney.

The tall gables in the right-hand part of the drawing may belong to the oldest part of the structure, which is unlikely to be earlier than 1200, while that part occupying much of the left-hand half of the picture has a core datable to around the thirteenth century. The buttresses of the gable and some of the nave walls belong to a later cladding added in the fifteenth century, which is probably the date of the unusual limestone tower with residence attached at the western end. This tower would have been the somewhat cramped abode of a curate, whose Dean would have lived in greater comfort closer to the ecclesiastical power centre in Limerick city.

Cooper noted in his diary of May 26th, 1781, that the tower had ruined battlements. He was careful to provide a small plan with measurements, and mentioned a large tomb in the east window, but he described the rest of the church as carrying 'very little marks of Antiquity on it's walls'.

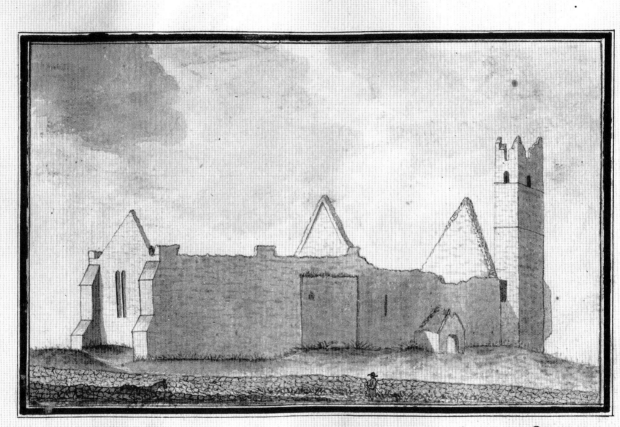

AC: delin. 26th May 1701 —   Pinxt 10th July —

Abbey of **Mungret** — Co. Limerick —

BLACK ABBEY, ADARE, Co. LIMERICK

A dare is a small town consisting of a few Cabbins; a small river called the Maige passes thro' it, over which is a plain bridge ... On the S.side of the river are the ruins of the abbey of Augustines ... The Choir is large, with stalls & ... N. of the steeple are the most beautiful Cloisters, with Gothic windows ... On most of these windows are escutcheons with the English & Saltire Cross's ... The workmanship here is very elegant – the principal parts, hewn Limestone, which looks quite fresh, & altogether gives it a modern, but awful appearance. Adjoining the Cloisters are several Appartments, wch. seem older than any of the other Parts.

This was Austin Cooper's diary entry for 26 May 1781, the day he visited Adare.

Adare has some of the best-preserved medieval buildings in the country. The Wyndham-Quin family, earls of Dunraven and former owners of these buildings, did much in the nineteenth century to preserve them – although in so doing they made certain changes, which occasionally have had their detractors. However, it should be acknowledged that the family are largely responsible for preventing further ruin.

The Black Abbey is a prime example of this – being now one of the very few medieval churches still in use anywhere in Ireland. The Dunravens gave the White, or Trinitarian, Abbey to the Catholic community in Adare, and the Black Abbey to the Protestant Church of Ireland, which continues to keep it in an exemplary manner.

John Fitz Thomas FitzGerald founded the Black Abbey in 1317 for the Augustinian Friars. Other than becoming Observant in 1472, its life was uneventful until it was dissolved around 1540. It was then found to possess several cottages and a fishing weir, which would have been an important source of food, as the friary was cleverly sited beside the River Maigue.

What Cooper's drawing shows is the western side of the 'convent', with the tower dominating the nave beneath it. Even in Cooper's day, the entrance doorway was blocked up, and today access is gained through a porch around the corner. To the right, as we look at it, is the twin-windowed gable of the south aisle while farther to the left is the western side of the domestic claustral buildings. This western view is not the most interesting aspect of the friary, but is valuable historically because it is here that the greatest changes have taken place.

Since Cooper's day, removal of the pervasive ivy has revealed a window above the nave doorway, which has now been totally blocked, and the double window of the same aisle has been replaced by a taller two-light Victorian Gothic window. But the most remarkable change is in the claustral buildings, which, in 1826, were replaced by the Wyndham-Quin family mausoleum. The gabled part on the left of this is now part of a school, which helps to make the whole building complex somewhat more alive than the usual ruins sketched by Cooper.

A.C. delin: 26: May 1781 —   Grav.d 11: July —

A W: View of the Black-Abbey at Adair Co. Limerick

ADARE CASTLE, Co. LIMERICK

Cooper needed only to walk about a hundred yards from where he sketched the Black Abbey (no.11), to reach the the bridge that provided his viewing-point for Adare Castle on the opposite side of the river. He himself, presumably, is the figure shown standing on the left-hand side. The ivy that covered much of the castle in his day made it into a most romantic ruin, and it has only been removed in recent years when Dúchas, Ireland's State Monument Service, took over the castle and began to conserve it – a process which is ongoing.

The first castle builder is unknown and, though generally called 'Desmond's Castle', it was held for much of the later medieval period by the Geraldine Earls of Kildare. Described by Killanin and Duignan's *Shell Guide to Ireland* as 'one of the most interesting examples of feudal architecture in the country', the castle consists of a not-quite-rectangular curtain wall, seen here in the left middle-ground, with entrance doorway. The wall encloses a tall, off-centre tower – the tallest ivy-covered building in the picture. The castle was built early in the thirteenth century, probably on the site of an earlier Norman earthen ring-work, and surrounded by a moat, now devoid of water.

Adare Castle is unique in Ireland in having two medieval banqueting halls, both with the long sides overlooking the River Maigue, which is seen flowing in the right foreground. One of these banqueting halls is seen covered in ivy to the right of the almost ivy-free crenellated tower, while the dark gable further to the right is a part of the second banqueting hall. Perhaps because it had taken him so long to sketch it, all Cooper had time to say about it in his diary was that it was 'a very large & strong Castle, said to be Desmond's'.

Like so many ruins in Ireland, its dilapidated state is attributed to the Cromwellians, whose countrywide swathe of destruction has been neither forgiven nor forgotten by the Irish people – and all those who love ancient buildings – over the last 350 years.

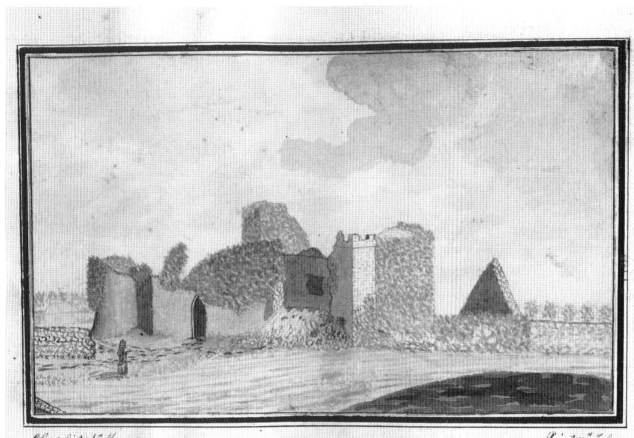

AC: delin.t 26.th May 1781   Sinx.t 11.th July

A S:W: View of Adair Castle, Co.y Limerich

CAPPAGH CASTLE, Co. LIMERICK

The sight of the tower of Cappagh Castle, just over two miles north-east of Rathkeale, must have caused Cooper to make a detour northwards from the Limerick–Tralee road while he was on his tour of Munster in 1781. His curiosity doubtless brought him along the bohereen where he portrayed himself looking at the castle to the east – one of the few pleasant instances where he includes himself in his pictures.

The castle was sited on a rock, which falls away more sharply than Cooper intimates, and the tall tower, which he places at the centre of his circular picture, stands alone in an inner bawn, or enclosure. The disappearance of its southern half has the advantage of showing us its cross-section. The tower is unusual in that there are three stone vaults, over the first, third and fourth floors respectively. Sadly, recent domestic burning activity has blackened some of the otherwise well-preserved basket-shuttering on the lowest of these.

Apart from its western side being built facing the cliff-face, the tower house is further fortified by the presence of an outer bawn, the northern part of which was converted into a ball alley several decades ago. Just beside it is the small rounded turret at the north-eastern angle seen on the left in Cooper's picture, and it is balanced on the south-eastern corner by a square turret.

The tower house itself was probably built by a Knight of Glin in the late fifteenth century, though the outermost wall – itself perhaps a later addition – is probably to be equated with the barbican, which, in 1591, was described as being 'ruined on the s(outh)'. Having been surrendered after a Confederate blockade in 1642, it comes as no surprise that the castle was described as 'ruined' thirteen years later. Local legend says that, in 1827, a FitzGerald of Ballyglehane Castle gave the use of Cappagh Castle to his brother who blew it up the day before he was to return it – supposedly at the insistence of the latter's wife.

Castle of Cappagh _ Co Limerick _

Taken from the Road _

with figure of Arth. Cooper.
1781

LISTOWEL CASTLE, Co. KERRY

Listowel Castle is the only monument in Co. Kerry represented among Austin Cooper's surviving drawings, though he may, of course, have done others that are now lost. He passed through the town the day after he visited Adare, Co. Limerick (nos.11–12), on his tour of Munster in 1781, iindicating that he was losing no time either in travelling or sketching.

Brooding over Listowel's square, Listowel Castle was a major feature in the town, which is better known nowadays for its literary associations and decoratively sculptured shops. The castle's history is inextricably linked with that of the Fitzmaurice family, the lords of the area since the thirteenth century. The Fitzmaurices or another prominent family, the McElligotts, were most likely the builders.

The castle was probably roughly square in shape, with an angular tower at each corner, though what we see today is merely one side of that square together with two of its corner towers. A modern observer can see light through some of the windows, because there is nothing behind them, but the darkness behind the openings in Cooper's drawing suggests that more of the castle survived 200 years ago. The very tall arch between the tops of the towers is so similar to that at Bunratty Castle that a mid-fifteenth century date for the castle would be quite reasonable.

Listowel was the last castle to hold out against the forces of Elizabeth I in the sixteenth century. Its Irish owners dismantled it in 1582 to prevent it falling into English hands, probably causing the loss of at least some of the castle. But in 1600, it surrendered to the Elizabethan army of Sir George Carew, under the command of Charles Wilmot, and its garrison of eighteen men were all executed. The eldest son of its owner, Lord Kerry, escaped, but the five-year-old was later captured through treachery, and the castle thereafter descended into oblivion.

The nearby River Feale is now further away from the back of the castle than is shown in Cooper's drawing.

A.C: delin.t 27.th May 1781.   Finis.t 13.th July

Castle of Listowel *Co.y Kerry*

ROUND TOWERS AT CLOYNE, CO CORK (A), AND CASHEL, CO TIPPERARY (B)

The Welshman Edward Lhuyd was one of the first to express pictorial interest in Round Towers, when he drew a fine example in Antrim town in 1699. In the same year this lucky individual was also present at the opening of the prehistoric passage grave at Newgrange.

Eighteenth- and nineteenth-century antiquarians were fascinated by Ireland's Round Towers. Dominating the Irish countryside, these free-standing ecclesiastical monuments were visible to all from a distance. But they retained the interest of onlookers through the years mainly because of the mystery associated with their function and origin.

Ideas about their use varied greatly – some believed that they were prehistoric or pagan, having been built by the Druids, the Danes or the Phoenicians, while others saw them as early observatories, fire temples or phallic symbols. But in the nineteenth century, the fact that they usually stand on early medieval monastic sites swung the debate strongly in the direction of a Christian use, be it as watch-towers, defensive citadels or – as implied by the name given them in the old Irish Annals, *clogthech* – bell-towers, or campaniles.

Not all Round Towers are in as good a state of preservation as these two, which are among the best in Ireland. The Cloyne tower withstood the force of a lightning storm on 10 January 1749, during which the local bishop – the famous George Berkeley – experienced what he described as the loudest thunderclap he had ever heard in Ireland. According to him, the arched vault on top of the tower was cracked, but despite falling down three storeys and shattering the door, the bell survived intact. This helps to explain the presence of the modern-looking broad doorway shown by Cooper and also perhaps the crenellations on top, which may have been added afterwards. The curious terrace, presumably functioning as a staircase, has since been removed – but the bell still peals for the cathedral nearby.

The Cashel tower looks svelte and slim when compared to the broader girth of the adjoining cathedral, which tends to engulf it somewhat. If its 92ft made it the tallest building on the Rock even after the cathedral was built in the thirteenth century, imagine how much more it must have dominated the surroundings when it was built in the eleventh or early twelfth century.

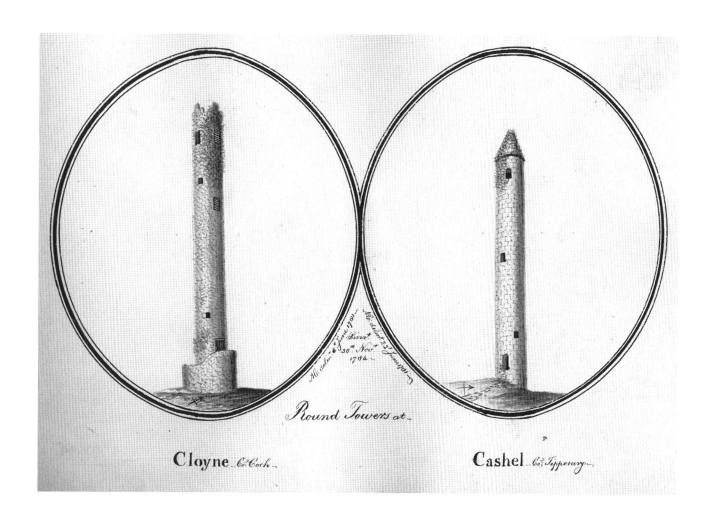

Round Towers at

Cloyne Co. Cork

Cashel Co. Tipperary

CLOYNE CASTLE, Co. CORK

On the same day – 8 June 1781 – that Austin Cooper sketched the Round Tower at Cloyne (no.15), he also took the opportunity of drawing Cloyne Castle in the town. We cannot but be grateful to him for his artistic energy because this is probably the only illustration we have of this urban tower house.

Cloyne Castle is likely to have had three storeys above the ground floor, lit largely through narrow window-slits and with irregular crenellations on the skyline. But, while it may have been built originally for defence, the large door and, more particularly, the lower windows suggest that it was later adapted for more commodious living. This may have happened shortly before Cooper sketched it, as the oriel window is an unexpected feature. If we follow Cooper's compass-bearing in the bottom left of the picture, the window must have faced north – so any extra light that it could bring into that side of the castle would have been welcome.

The adjoining domestic buildings – one single-storeyed and probably thatched, and the other two-storeyed – stand at right angles to one another, flush with the two visible sides of the castle. This positioning suggests that they stood at the crossroads in the middle of the village, not far from the Round Tower. Since in the medieval period Cloyne was a bishopric, not a walled town, it would seem that it was in the castle that the manor court of the bishops was held. It may well be that parts of the old castle survive, still embedded in one of the houses of the town.

ℋℰ: delin.ᵗ 8.ᵗʰ June 1781 —   Piᵗⁿ.ᵗ 17.ᵗʰ July —

Castle of **Cloyne** Cᵒ.ᵗʰ Cork

CASTLE MARY, Co. CORK

For Austin Cooper, 8 June 1781 must have been a very busy day. Not only did he draw Cloyne Round Tower and Castle (nos.15–16), but he also drew a 'cromliagh' at Castle Mary, a mile and a half to the west, where he was probably the guest of the Longfield family.

The Longfields had apparently had a medieval castle here but, by Cooper's time, it had been re-worked, almost certainly by the well-known Sardinian architect Davis Duckart. It was subsequently transformed into a pseudo-Tudor mansion in the nineteenth century, before being set on fire during the Civil War and left the gaunt ruin it now is.

On the outskirts of the wooded part of the demesne stands the cromliagh (spelled 'cromlech' in old maps), a word derived from the Welsh term for a crooked or circular stone. Today we would call it a dolmen (a term taken, curiously, from the cognate language, Breton, and meaning a 'stone table').

The monument itself consists of a heavy, flattish capstone. One end is on the ground, and it is tilted in the air so that the other end is supported by upright stones, one of which is now fallen. Adjacent to it is a recumbent stone shown on the left by Cooper, who makes it look almost like an oyster shell. The presence of two stunted, and now vanished, trees – not dissimilar to bonsai – on top of the capstone give the monument a surreal appearance, almost as if it had come out of an Hieronymus Bosch painting.

Its prehistoric origins were doubted by Ruaidhrí de Valera and Seán Ó Nualláin, who left it out of the *Megalithic Survey* (1982). However, as there is no reason to see it as a folly set up in Austin Cooper's own century, it should probably be accepted as a genuine Stone Age dolmen, even if it does not quite correspond to what we expect a dolmen to look like.

A Cromliagh at Castle-Mary Co⁷ Cork

EAST WINDOW, ST MARY'S CHURCH, YOUGHAL, Co. CORK

As the distinguished architectural historian, Maurice Craig, pointed out, St Mary's Protestant church in the Cork seaport town of Youghal would be unremarkable among the many ancient Gothic parish churches in England. However, it stands out in an Irish context because it is the second largest medieval parish church still in use in Ireland.

While St Mary's may contain elements of an earlier structure, the nave in its present form is no earlier than the thirteenth century, when Richard Bennet and his wife Ellis Barry, both members of distinguished Norman families in Cork, gave money for the church to be built. Its most unusual feature is the impressive wooden roof that has protected the nave for hundreds of years.

But the window that Cooper drew is the pride and glory of the choir. It was added around 1464 when Thomas, the seventh earl of Desmond, established a college to supply the church services, thus making it into a collegiate church. The measurements of 26ft x 15ft 6in, which Cooper gives beneath, indicate just how sizeable the window is. We know nothing of the glass that once decorated it, as the whole church was wrecked in 1579 when the rebel sixteenth earl of Desmond and his soldiers destroyed vestments, chalices and other furniture while stabling their horses within the church. Yet the stonework tracery, framed like a number of flickering candles rising to embrace a rosette at the top, withstood the vandals and, with the help of a mid-nineteenth century re-roofing of the choir, has survived intact to our own day.

The window is now filled with modern glass which, when seen in conjunction with the recent effective installation of internal lighting, can transform the interior into a joyous place in which to wander and to pray. It is the first feature of the church to strike the visitor entering the churchyard gates, beside the house where Sir Walter Raleigh is reported to have lived. It certainly creates a remarkable impression on part of the exterior choir walls, which have recently been cleaned to great advantage, making the whole church an enticing place to visit.

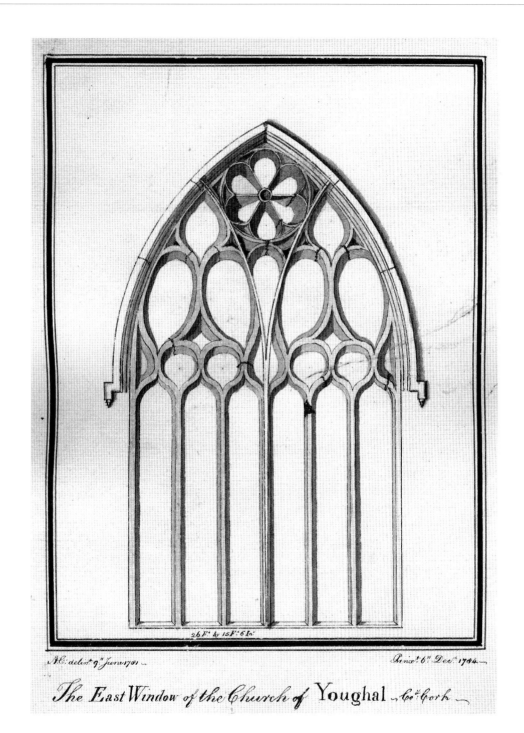

26 F.ᵗ by 15 F.ᵗ 6 Iᵗ

A.C. delin.ᵗ 9ᵗʰ June 1791.

Pinx.ᵗ 6ᵗʰ Dec.ᵗ 1744.

The East Window of the Church of Youghal *Co.ᵗ Cork*

NORTH ABBEY, YOUGHAL, Co. CORK

Youghal was an important maritime centre in the medieval period, when its ships, trading as far away as Spain, brought prosperity and people to the town. Their religious needs were catered for not only in St Mary's (no.18), but also in the foundations of both Franciscans and Dominicans. It was for the latter Order that Thomas Fitzmaurice founded the friary of St Mary of Thanks at the northern end of the town around the year 1268. This friary subsequently rose to such importance that general chapters of the Irish branch of the Order were held here in 1281 and 1304.

The gable, which Cooper drew on his way from Cloyne on 9 June 1781, may date back to the thirteenth century, but the three-light window has the air of a fifteenth-century

addition. As in Cooper's day, the gable stands alone and the ruin he mentions as standing 'about 32 yards distant' is not quite part of the east window as he suggests but, more probably, part of the east window of the south aisle of the church.

Both of the remaining parts of the friary stand somewhat forlornly in the middle of a graveyard, a sad reminder of the importance of this foundation which, after being dissolved around 1540, was acquired by Sir Walter Raleigh in 1587. Its greatest treasure was a small ivory carving of Our Lady of Graces – reflecting the title of the monastery – which is now preserved in the Dominican church of St Mary in Cork city.

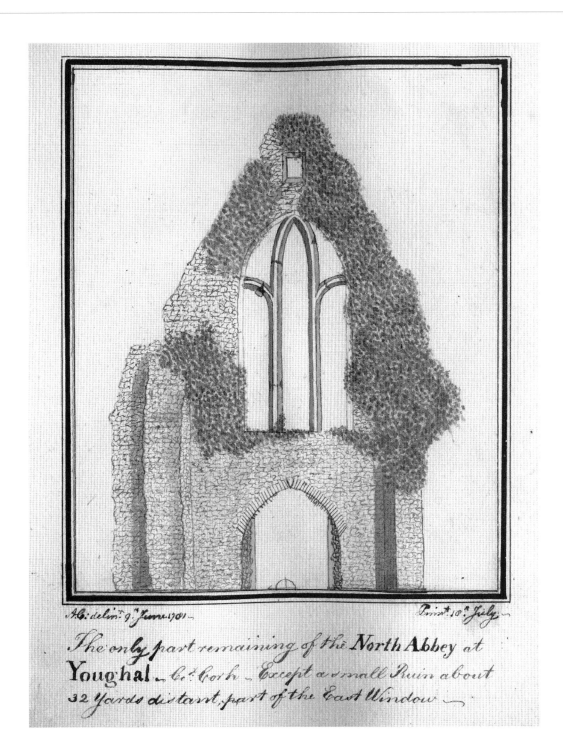

AC: delin.t 9.th June 1781.   Print.d 10.th July

The only part remaining of the North Abbey at
Youghal _ Co.t Cork _ Except a small Ruin about
32 Yards distant, part of the East Window

LISMORE BRIDGE, Co. WATERFORD

W here the Ferry formerly was over the river here, a new & elegant bridge has been built, whereon is this inscription:

A:D: 1777
This bridge was built at
the sole expence of his Grace
William Duke of Devonshire.

On the N. side of the river are 11 plain arches, on Acct. of the low situation of the ground, from which to the opposite bank, is thrown over the river (the rest dry, except in floods) one great arch, the Chord whereof is 102 feet, & to the crown of the arch only 25 ft. – the whole height from the Top to the present level of the water 43 feet.

Mr. Connor the Duke's Agent who resides in the Castle, informed me, that it cost his Grace to the Architects, exclusive of some other expenses, £7,200. It was designed by Mr. Ivory, & executed by Messrs. Darley, & Stokes.

This is Austin Cooper's commentary on the bridge spanning the River Blackwater at Lismore in Co. Waterford. For someone whose main hobby was drawing antiquities, it is perhaps surprising to find him including in his album a utilitarian monument only four years old. But this clearly shows in what reverence Ivory's achievement was held by contemporaries – not to mention the amount of money that an absentee landlord was prepared to pay for the public to cross the river in full sight of his castle.

In Cooper's day, the castle was a sprawling ruin and it was not until about seventy years later that one of the duke's successors got Joseph Paxton – of Crystal Palace fame – to remodel it into its present fairy-tale form above the leafy River Blackwater. According to O'Keeffe and Simington's book *Irish Stone Bridges,* the Lismore arch was probably inspired by the 60ft span of the structure built across the River Lee in 1766 – which it managed almost to double. Even in 1879, the only Irish bridge larger than it was that over the Liffey at Island-bridge, which out-spanned it by a mere 4ft.

Ivory's bridge was not only a triumph of engineering, it was also a masterpiece of bridge design, which withstood a disastrous flood on the Blackwater in 1853. This flood was probably the reason why some of the six other arches on the north side of the bridge (not shown) had to be repaired in 1858, as an inscription states. Ivory's design is elegant, with what looks like pedimented corner turrets and round-headed recesses below.

Thomas Ivory (*c.*1732–86) designed two of Dublin's major buildings, the Bluecoat School in Blackhall Place (now the Incorporated Law Society) and the Newcomen Bank, now owned by Dublin Corporation, with one side facing Dublin Castle and the other the Royal Exchange (now City Hall). Dr Edward McParland has described Ivory's designs for the school as 'the loveliest architectural drawings produced in Ireland in the eighteenth century'. When we take on board his further judgement that Ivory was 'the greatest Irish architect of the 1770s', we can readily understand why Cooper decided to deviate from his norm of just drawing ruins to illustrate Lismore Bridge in his album.

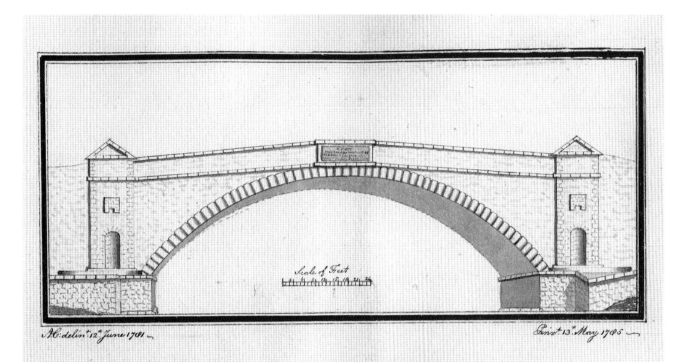

A.C. delin.t 12.th June 1781

Const.d 13.th May 1785

Scale of Feet

The Great Arch of Lismore Bridge — Co.ty Waterford

CARRICKBEG TOMB, Co. WATERFORD

Ever since the construction of Newgrange in Co. Meath and the Pyramids at Giza, humankind has been trying to overcome 'Death the great leveller' by creating monuments that keep alive the memory of the (affluent) dead.

Today, we frequently see a photograph of the deceased attached to a headstone. But in medieval western Europe, the way to ensure that posterity would not forget you too quickly was to have a stone effigy of yourself carved after – or, preferably, before – your death. The Ancient Greeks and Romans did this too, but whereas they placed *upright* the stone carvings bearing the likeness of the dead, the effigies of the second Christian millennium tended to be placed *horizontally*, lying flat over the grave of the deceased.

When the Normans came to Ireland, they brought with them this practice of having their effigies placed above their tombs and sometimes, one suspects, they even brought the effigy already carved with them from the other side of the Irish Sea.

This may have been the case with the effigy that Austin Cooper sketches at Carrickbeg, which overlooks the River Suir on the bank opposite Carrick-on-Suir. Underneath a rather angular arch in relief rests a figure with a long gown splaying in pleats beneath the waist, and wearing over it what appears to be a cloak, the ends of which can be seen to fall down to ankle-level at either side. The effigy may well be that of a lady, dating perhaps from the period after 1336 when the church was founded. Sadly, not a trace of the figure survives today.

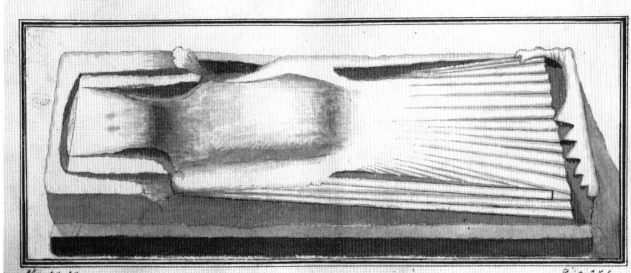

Alg.t delin.t 17.th June 1701 —   Pinx.t 19.th July —

An Old Tomb in the Abbey of **Carrick-beg** — Co.y Waterford —

FRANCISCAN FRIARY, CASHEL, Co. TIPPERARY

Having discussed what he found on his visit to Hore Abbey in Cashel (nos.8–9), Cooper notes the following event in a rather matter-of-fact way in his diary:

> 1757. Feby. 14th. At night the lofty & beautiful steeple of St. Francis Abby., fell to the ground without any other mischief than terrifying the Inhabitants with it's prodigious noise ... It fell perpendicularly when all the parts separated without the least appearance of cement wch. was occasioned by there being too much loam in the Composition.

He goes on to describe Hacket's Abbey as being 'so far destroyed that no distinction can be made of it's several parts' and that it was 150ft long and 25ft broad. There was a small chapel with handsome window on the south side and a 'low, deep vault' on the north side and, he continues:

> When I was viewing this place, Mr Kyffin, had men at work pulling it down for the stones, particularly those of the east window. In 1795 the small remains of this Abbey were completely removed, & on the Scite a Popish Chapel built.

When Cooper visited Cashel on 20 June 1781, he sketched all that remained of the friary. What he reveals to us is a long, hall church, with traces of a set of lancet windows in the east gable, on the left. The south wall of the nave is, equally, perforated by a series of five lancet windows – there were doubtless originally more – and there is an arched building on the left, as in the Franciscan friary in Ennis, which shares many features with the Cashel friary. The fragment of the west end with rounded (and blocked) arcade, and the addition of a south chapel with traceried windows, represent further similarities with Ennis. The tower, which had fallen twenty-six years previously to leave the small, flat, jagged platform in the centre foreground, may also have been an addition, as it was in Ennis.

Cooper's visit to sketch the friary was timely, because the work of Mr Kyffin, who is illustrated with his pickaxe pulling down the east window, was shortly afterwards to leave, literally, 'not a stone upon a stone'.

AC. delin.t 20.th June 1791

Pinx.t 20.th July

The Friery of Conventual Franciscans in Cashel, reformed to Observantines. Co.ty Tipperary

ATHASSEL ABBEY, Co. Tipperary

Cooper must have ridden out at the summer solstice of 1781 and sat down on the sward overlooking Athassel Abbey near the village of Golden, letting his horse graze untethered while he relaxed with his sketching pad. Opposite, we can see him from behind admiring the ancient ruin which, in his own words:

> shows by it's present Remains, the noble building it has been; & equals, if not surpasses, most in this Kingdom of Monastic Edifices.

Cooper gives quite a lengthy description of the buildings, along with measurements, before adding:

> to particularize every other part of this extensive Abbey would be altogether as disagreable to a reader as a writer.

This suggests that, as he wrote his diary, he knew he would not be the only one to read it.

The abbey had been built by William de Burgo around 1200 and was confirmed by King John of England in 1205. The monastery, consisting of a large nave and chancel church with tall tower linking the two and an extensive cloister garth, together with outbuildings, was located on an island in the River Suir. It was reachable by a bridge that still exists. Access was through a gate lodge, which survives but which Cooper could not fit in on the left of his picture. The perspective of the abbey is rather distorted in order to show particular features.

Nevertheless the picture demonstrates the scale of the buildings and their ruined state, the latter having been accomplished by two separate raids on the monastery – one by the Norman John FitzThomas in 1319 and the other by the Irish Brian O'Brien ten years later.

Cooper's drawing of Athassel was engraved by Ledwich a decade later in Grose's *Antiquities of Ireland* – probably the only large composition of Cooper's to have been so treated in his lifetime.

A.C. delin.t 22.d June 1781.

Const 21.st July.

A N.W. View of Athaffel Abbey — Co.y Tipperary

EFFIGY AT ATHASSEL ABBEY, Co. TIPPERARY

In the Abbey of Athassel, Austin Cooper found in the choir 'an Old Tomb of a Woman, so covered with rubbish, that I could scarcely draw any part of it'. He did, however, make an attempt, and has left us the tall, unsigned drawing opposite.

The body of the figure is at present backing on to the south wall of the choir. The head is covered in wavy hair – which misled Cooper into thinking that this was the effigy of a woman –and he seems to indicate that it had been severed from the body when he drew it more than two centuries ago. Today, the head still sits awkwardly, but it is in reality the head of a man, and it probably originally belonged to the torso now beneath it. What appears to be an amulet hanging around the neck is more likely to have been a ring-brooch – a type of jewellery (recently studied by Mary B Deevy), which was worn on the breast by both

men and women to link two sides of a tunic. Here, a mantle falling from the left shoulder is grasped waist-high by the figure's left hand, and he appears to hold a glove in his right. The main garment is a long gown that falls in drapes to the ground and is held by a girdle at the waist.

The late John Hunt, a great connoisseur of medieval dress and armour, suggested that the figure may have been carved around 1270–1280. This date fits in well with the suggested identification of the figure as one Walter de Burgo, a member of the monastery's founding family, who died in Galway in 1271 and was brought to Athassel for burial.

Cooper's drawing was used by his cousin Joseph Cooper Walker to illustrate his book *Historical Essay on the Dress of the Ancient and Modern Irish,* published in London in 1788.

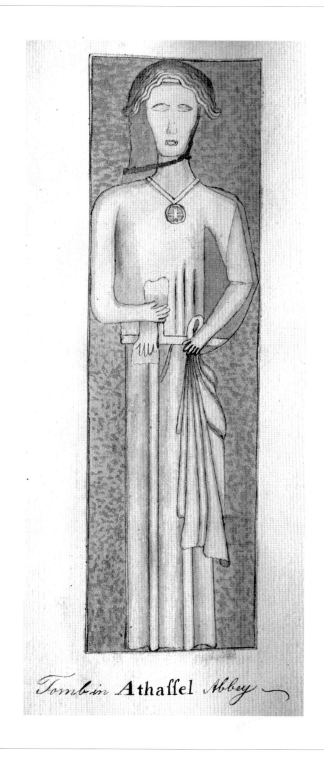

Tomb in Athassel Abbey

URLINGFORD CASTLE, Co. KILKENNY

On 26 June 1781, while searching for castles standing along the Dublin–Cashel road, Austin Cooper noted the following:

> Urlingford, is a very poor Village, situated in a Bog. A small Castle here surrounded by a wall, with towers, two of wch. only remain – near it, the ruins of a very old Church.

The castle still stands, at least in part. However, the buildings at right and left of the actual tower have disappeared, though an outhouse may contain the remains of the building with sloping roof, shown here on the right by Cooper. The corners of the tower were eroded even in 1781, and only a part of the twin windows on the upper floor survive. Much of the east wall – which Cooper shows in shadow just to the right of centre – has also disappeared, as have most of the west and north walls.

The present owner, Mr Stanley, who runs a garage beside the castle, maintains that there was a stone bearing the date 1605, which is now lost. This lost stone may well indicate the date of the construction of the castle – placing it thus late in the series of Irish tower houses, which goes back to the fifteenth century, if not earlier.

The Mill Cemetery nearby is probably the location of the 'very old church' referred to by Cooper. A note on the castles in the Freshford district, published in the very first volume of *Transactions of the Kilkenny Archaeological Society* in 1849–51, suggests that this castle was formerly a stronghold of the Mountgarrett family.

AC: delin.t 26.th June 1781 —   Pinx.t 22.d July —

Castle of Urlingford — Co.y Kilkenny —

DOMINICAN ABBEY, NAAS, Co. KILDARE

Writing of the town of Naas in his diary of 27 June 1781, Austin Cooper noted that:

On the N. side is the ruins of the Dominican Abbey founded by the Eustace's – of it remains, a small square steeple supported on an arch & adjoining on the N: side, are the side walls; of what part I cannot say; but a more ruinous pile, I never yet have seen.

Yet Cooper's drawing, reproduced opposite, does not make it look quite so ruinous. The tower – or steeple as he called it – was obviously solidly built and well preserved, perhaps because it was a late – and independent – insertion into a much older building. The tall wall seen on the left beside it, being two-storey, may well have been part of the domestic buildings of the friars-preachers attached to the church. The whole was, apparently, demolished in 1835, and Cooper's picture is probably the only surviving drawing of this, once important, Dominican house.

The priory bore the name of St Eustace – a rather unusual dedicatee until it is remembered that it was the Eustace or FitzEustace family who founded the house around 1355. This was only a few years after the horrible scourge of the Black Death, which must have wrought havoc among the citizens of Naas.

Little is known of the priory's subsequent history until the Reformation, when it was suppressed. At that time, it possessed ten gardens, eleven acres of land, a water mill and five cottages. To have been able to build up such assets would suggest that the priory must have been economically affluent over a long period.

AC: delin.t 27.th June 1781.   Pinx.t 22.d July.

Dominican Abbey at Naas, Co. Kildare

MOTTES AT KILMORONY (A) AND TIMAHOE (B), CO. LAOIS, AND RATOATH (C), CO. MEATH

Presented as if painted on three separate scraps of torn paper with rolled-up or folded sides or corners, these drawings are actually grouped together on one sheet. Cooper was, as it happens, quite correct in doing this, since these monuments would now all be classed as mottes – flat-topped mounds resembling Christmas puddings, which date from the later twelfth or early thirteenth century.

It was the historian Goddard Orpen who first recognised Irish mottes as the fortifications of the earliest Norman invaders, erected by great barons or their tenants to establish a military foothold in recently conquered territories. A motte was often accompanied by a bailey – an adjoining flat area of ground protected by an earthen wall and ditch, and designed to provide defended space for both soldiers and livestock. On the flat top of the mound we should imagine the former presence of a bretesche, a wooden lookout tower. Inevitably, traces of the bretesche have disappeared.

Cooper has chosen to illustrate examples from the eastern province of Leinster, where more than half of the 450 or so surviving Irish mottes are located. That at Kilmoroney (or, more correctly, Kilmorony), in Co. Laois, he sketched from across the River Barrow at Grangemellon, Co. Kildare. Even at a distance of a good few hundred yards, the 28ft-high motte appears to loom out of the undulating landscape. It is surrounded by a ditch, which was once water-filled, and has a bailey to the west, scarcely visible in Cooper's drawing.

The second motte is in the townland of Ballinaclogh Lower, about a mile south-west (*not* south-east as Cooper has indicated) of Timahoe in Co. Laois. It is surrounded on three sides by a ditch with a bank outside it, and was probably the 'castle of Timahoe' that Giraldus Cambrensis, the Welsh historian, described as having been built for Meiler FitzHenry by Hugh de Lacy, Lord of Meath. De Lacy's expertise in building fortresses farther north may have been needed in shaping this monument of Norman penetration in Laois. Quarrying operations on the esker ridge on which it stands was threatening its very existence up to the late 1980s, when a preservation order was placed on it to allow archaeological excavation to take place. As it transpired, the finds turned out to be later than medieval.

The most impressive of the three mottes is at Ratoath, Co. Meath. This motte is now in the grounds of a Catholic church, and stands to a height of more than 30ft, with a diameter of almost 200ft. The few miserable trees of Cooper's day have spread to such an extent that much of the mound is now wooded, and some of the banks seem to have been replaced by hedges. The house on the left, perhaps the predecessor of the present parochial house, is now gone. In the churchyard on the opposite side of the road there is the effigy of an unidentified knight, presumably a member of the same family for whom the motte was raised.

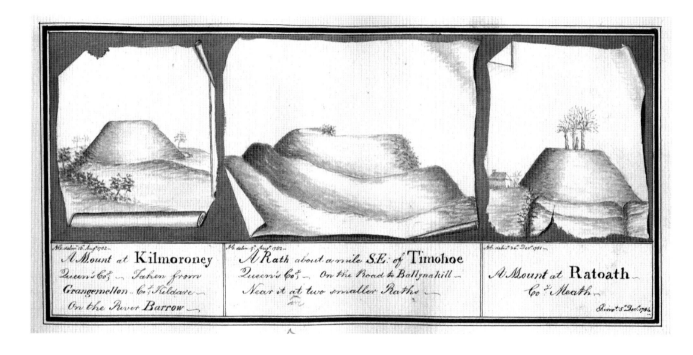

No. dedn. 18 Augt 1792.

A Mount at **Kilmoroney**
Queen's Coy. Taken from
Grangemellon Coy. Kildare
On the River **Barrow**

No. dedn. 9 Augt 1782.

A **Rath** *about a mile S.E. of* **Timohoe**
Queen's Coy. On the Road to Ballynakill
Near it at two smaller Raths

No. exhibt 24 Decr 1761.

A Mount at **Ratoath**
Coy. Meath

Exra 5 Decr 1794.

DUNMORE CASTLE, Co. GALWAY

There is something Christmas card-like in the way this picture shows a coach-and-four on a road leading to a bridge with a romantic castle ruin in the background – deep, white snow is the only thing missing! But on closer inspection we see that the coach is not in motion, but stationary; its open door makes us look towards the bridge over the Sinking River where the passenger is seen drawing the gaunt shell of a castle.

The fragmentary remains of the outer curtain wall in front of the artist once protected the castle. The tall and impressive building, apparently sitting on a hill, may, in fact, be resting upon an earlier Norman motte. Indeed, one might well wonder if it were not erected on the site of one of the few castles known to have been built in Ireland *before* the Norman invasion by the O'Conor kings of Connacht? After all, it is known that it was at Dunmore that Ireland's mightiest twelfth-century High King, Turlough O'Conor (1119–56), had his fortified residence. The Normans moved into central Connacht around 1225, and the lower parts of the castle as it stands may have been built by the de Berminghams at the behest of the de Burgos in that year.

The castle may be described as a two-storey hall keep with a grand hall on the first floor, accessible only through an external timber stairway, similar to a castle at Athenry, Co. Galway, that the de Berminghams built in 1238. But the castle owes much of its present appearance to alterations made around the fifteenth century when two more storeys were added to make the castle into a tower house. At that time the de Burgos had lost some of the power that Dunmore Castle had helped them accrue in Connacht. However, the de Berminghams managed to retain possession of the castle as late as the seventeenth century.

There are some indications that the castle was lived in until the nineteenth century, and William Ouseley – the man who made the original drawing that Cooper copied in this illustration – was actually born in the castle in 1771.

Wil.^m Ousley delin^t March 1782 —

H. Pine^t 9.th April 1782 —

A Perspective View of Dunmore Castle *Co.^y Galway —*

THE GODS OF THE NEALE, Co. MAYO

The medieval stones assembled together above an inscription and known collectively as 'The Gods of the Neale' are among the most curious and mysterious in the west of Ireland. They are located in the village of The Neale (from the Irish *An Aill*, meaning rock), the former demesne of Lord Kilmaine, and they stand close to the entrance opposite the modern village school.

On the top of the monument is a ball, now broken off, standing on a pedestal – perhaps originally the base of a cross. The pedestal bears a Gothic Black Letter inscription of 1526 asking a prayer for one David O'Minahan, or Moran, and his wife Duoreen, or Norina.

Beneath the plinth upon which the pedestal stands are three sculpted panels, perhaps all originally from the same monument. These date from the late fifteenth century, and show one animal rampant, another standing and a human figure.

What seems to be a blank occupying the upper part of the square base beneath these figures is, in fact, a large stone with a long and partially incomprehensible inscription, possibly erected by Sir John Browne, a friend of Lord Charlemont's, in 1753. Its first paragraph is as follows, and presumably refers to the Black Letter inscription:

> The Irish characters on the above stone impart that in this cave we have by us the gods of Coins, Borderiss (?).

> Let us follow their stepps, sicke of love, with full confidence in Loo: Lave Adda Va?Kene, the Shepherd of Ireland:of his ERA AN: DI.

The 'Loo:Lave Adda' is a reference to Lugh Lamh-fada, the benign, long-armed god of the ancient Celts, who is the subject of a long discussion in the third paragraph (not reproduced here) where he is described as having 'founded the druids'.

The second paragraph of the inscription, which refers to the animals and human figure in the three panels, is as follows:

> These images were found in a cave behind the place they now stand, and were the ancient gods of the Neale which took its name from them. They were called Diane Ffeale, or the gods of Fellicity, from which the place in Irish was called Neheale, in English The Neale.

The inscription and the whole monument should be seen not just as a piece of romantic dilettante erudition, but also as an extraordinary piece of reverence to the Celtic past by a member of the landed aristocracy in the west of Ireland. This was at a time when many would have considered such reverence neither 'popular nor profitable', to use Myles na gCopaleen's immortal phrase.

Wil^m Ousley delin.^t   Ath.stone 12th April 1782

Temple at the **Neal** *— Co.^t Mayo.*

Inscription Flag 5:6 long, 5f.^t high

ANCHORET'S TOWERS AT OUGHTERARD, CO. KILDARE (A), KILMACDUAGH, CO. GALWAY (B), AND DISERT, CO. LAOIS (C)

On 20 May 1782, Austin Cooper noted in his diary that he 'rode to Aughterard Church, took a drawing of it and tower'. In this drawing, seen on the left of the trio opposite, he gives it the more usual spelling Oughterard. He was not referring to the well-known place of that name in Co. Galway, but instead to a small isolated group of monuments, consisting of a church and Round Tower, located north-east of Kill in Co. Kildare, about a mile and a half north of the modern Naas–Dublin dual carriageway. Both church and tower are illustrated overleaf (no.31), but here the tower is allowed to stand on its own. Cooper describes it as:

> About 25 feet high – it's circumference is 48 feet – the wall 3 feet thick – the door faces nearly E. 5 feet high, 2 feet broad at the bottom, the top arched and narrowed, and about 8 feet from the present level of the ground, which is evidently raised – the inside is divided into stories by a projection of the Stones of which only five remain, the lower mostly filled up, and the upper much broken on one side and quite open at the top – the door is finished with County of Dublin Mountain stone and on the inside is a mortise in the stone for a bolt.

In calling this an 'Anchoret's tower', Cooper was echoing current antiquarian views in a debate that was to run for centuries as to the purpose and use of Round Towers. The name given was possibly associating them with the pillars atop which early Christian anchorites like Simon Stylites sat for decades.

The tower at Kilmacduagh, in the centre of the picture opposite, Cooper copied from a drawing signed R Ousley, most likely Ralph (later Sir Ralph) Ouseley, who was a brother of William Ouseley (see no.28). He was born at Dunmore, Co. Galway in 1770, so that he was only 21 when he did the drawing of this tower at the southern extremity of his own home county. He was to go on to become an Ambassador to the Court of Persia and an Oriental scholar. Kilmacduagh is one of the best preserved of all the Irish Round Towers, with a doorway almost 25ft above ground. It has a tilt of about 2° out of the vertical, a fact not shown in Cooper's drawing, though the angle of the ground helps to indicate that the lean was present even in Cooper's day.

The third tower at Disert, Co. Laois, was obviously circular. But Cooper rightly suspected that this one would not have fitted into the definition of the usual Irish Round Tower when he wrote in his diary of 9 August 1782 that: 'I really suppose from it's appearance to have been a windmill & not an Anchoret's tower'.

Cooper grouped all three towers into an attractively shaped tableau that he painted on 4 March 1785.

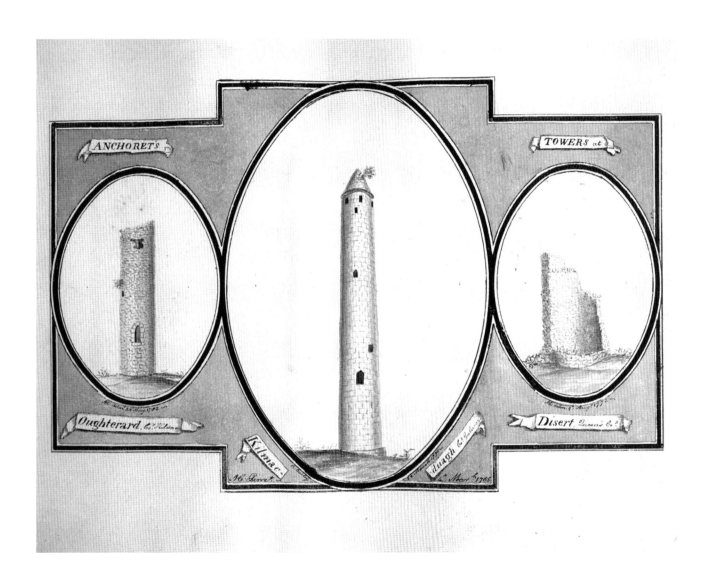

ANCHORETS TOWERS at

Oughterard, Co. Kildare

Kilmac... duagh Co. Galway

Disert, Queen's Co.

4.th March 1765

OUGHTERARD CHURCH and ROUND TOWER, Co. KILDARE

Cooper returns again to the Anchoret's tower at Oughterard, Co. Kildare (no.30), in this drawing, but this time he includes the church on the site. He covered both in his unusually lengthy description of this pair of monuments as follows:

> The Church of Aughterard is delightfully situated on a beautiful hill commanding a most pleasing and extensive prospect. It's present state is very ruinous and appears equally ancient. A small arched porch on the south west angle leads into the church which is small, and on the E. end is a Saxon arch, leading into the chancel which is arched over, with a small triple window on the East end – a small square tower like a Buttress on the South side leads to that part over the chancel now quite open and without any lateral walls.

There follows a further description of the tower already quoted in no.30, after which Cooper continues:

> The whole, both of Church and tower, is built of a greyish slaty stone found on that ground, and the cases of the doors and windows are finished with a red Grit or Freestone, as most old buildings in this Kingdom are.

> Tradition says this place has been of some note – 14 great Inns are said to have been at Aughterard. The Castle and a large tract of country here, formerly belonged to the family of the Cavanaghs; and some of the family until of late years lived in the Castle, which we may naturally suppose was their Mansion, and of course built by them. Should one judge of it's former prosperity by it's present state, no favourable hopes could be entertained of it's Greatness. However, that is not a Rule observed by Antiquaries.

It should be added that Cooper's 'small square tower like a Buttress on the South side' has since become detached from the main fabric of the church, and would long have fallen had it not been carefully supported on the outside.

The porch that Cooper mentions is no longer functional, having been replaced by a hemispherical mound. Its internal doorway is now blocked by a stone announcing that 'in the adjoining vault are deposited the mortal remains of Arthur Guinness late of James's Gate in the city and of Beaumont in the County of Dublin, Esquire, who departed this life on the 23rd of January A.D. 1803 aged 78 years … '. This esteemed personage is none other than Uncle Arthur, whose signature goes out daily on millions of cans and bottles of 'the black stuff' that originated in the famous brewery he founded in 1759. It is, perhaps, appropriate that he should find his eternal rest at a place which once had '14 great Inns', and it is probably in his honour that the churchyard is so immaculately kept today – a pleasant development from the way Cooper found it almost 220 years ago.

AC delint 20ᵗ May 1782   Pinxt 23ᵗ May

The Church & Tower of **Oughterard** Coy Kildare

ST WOLSTAN'S, NEAR CELBRIDGE, CO. KILDARE

The five monuments that Cooper drew at St Wolstan's near Celbridge are presented to us as if each were on a separate scroll of paper, ragged at the edges, curled up at the corners, and unrolled for our edification. This device is very appropriate under the circumstances, as all five stand in a somewhat higgledy-piggledy fashion around a very large field on the Celbridge side of St Wolstan's, a seventeenth- or eighteenth-century house probably owned by Dr Bernard, Bishop of Killaloe, when Cooper paid two visits, once in May 1781, and again in the same month the following year.

With the exception of the tower on the bottom left, which has disappeared, things are much the same as in Cooper's day, though some changes can be reported. The heavy covering of ivy on the bottom right has now gone, revealing a window restored probably within the last hundred years. As if to make up for this, the upper part of the building at top right is now smothered in ivy. What is remarkable is that three out of the four surviving buildings are gateways. The gateway on the bottom right has living quarters attached, and was originally approached through the gateway on the top left, which now stands somewhat forlorn in the middle of the field.

Further residential quarters were provided by the tower in the centre of the upper row, which was repaired with new window surrounds in the nineteenth century, when an unexpected, but damaged, figure of an angel in white marble was inserted over the south doorway (a side that is not seen in Cooper's picture).

These monuments and, in particular, the gateways, give an inkling of the importance of the monastery to which they once gave access. The monastery was founded by Richard, its first prior, and Adam de Hereford in 1202 for the Augustinian canons of St Victor, who we shall meet again at Newtown Trim (no.84). The monastery tried to escape the clutches of Archbishop Alen, who had been entrusted by King Henry VIII with the task of its suppression, and, for its pains, got as its new owner John Alen, the Lord Chancellor, whose family remained in possession for more than two centuries.

For a monastery that was found to possess gardens, mills, rectories, and more than 1,000 acres at the time of the Reformation, it is surprising that so little remains. There must, at the very least, have been a large church and claustral buildings acting as the centrepiece to the buildings drawn here by Cooper.

6. May 1781

6. May 1784

. May 1782

20 May 1782

20 May 1782

No finisd 26. May 1782

Ruins of the Priory of St Wolstan. Co^t Kildare

ANCHORET'S TOWERS AT TIMAHOE, CO. LAOIS (A), AND CASTLEDERMOT (B) AND OLD KILCULLEN (C), CO. KILDARE

The three Round Towers of Timahoe (or Timohoe, as Cooper spelled it), Castledermot and Old Kilcullen, which Cooper sketched on three different days in the August of 1782, were obviously regarded by him as 'Anchoret's towers' (see no.30) to judge by the title he gave to the drawing.

Timahoe is one of the finest, and certainly the most decorative, of all the Irish Round Towers, with a beautifully carved Romanesque doorway, and is described by Cooper as follows:

> Timohoe … is remarkable for a fine Round Tower, in good preservation, the top or cap is broken, the wall 4 ft 4 ins. Thick – the inside Diamr. 9 ft. , consequently it's external Circumfe. is abt. 53 ft. or 17 yards 2/3. The inside is divided into 7 stories by six rings of Rests formed by a conical inclination of each story, (as in many others) except the 2d. which is of projecting stones & even with the door.

He continues by talking about the doorway:

> … finely finished with the old crenellated Ornament, supported by clustered pillasters & hieroglyphical Capitals, altogether one of the most perfect specimens of our ancient Architecture I have seen in the Kingdom.

The tower at Castledermot is unusual in having crenellations at the top. Unfortunately the roof and weather vane, not to mention the ivy, shown in Cooper's drawing, have all disappeared since he drew the tower and gave the following short description:

> About 3 yards N. of the church stands a large Round Tower now used as a Belfry; I could neither measure it or get to see it's inside, as the entrance is by a door in a small building joining it to the church, which was locked.

Cooper sketched the tower dominating the skyline at Old Kilcullen and gave a detailed description of it, ending with the remark that:

> The tower is in a very ruinous state & will probably be soon added to the prostrate ruins of Kilcullen. A pity! As it is a fine landmark.

His fears have fortunately not come to pass, as only the narrower top of the tower is no longer extant. Cooper obviously spent some time at Old Kilcullen, as he gives details of a knight's effigy (see no.39), the shaft of a High Cross, and a disappeared church with Romanesque doorway, of which an excavation in 1939 revealed few traces.

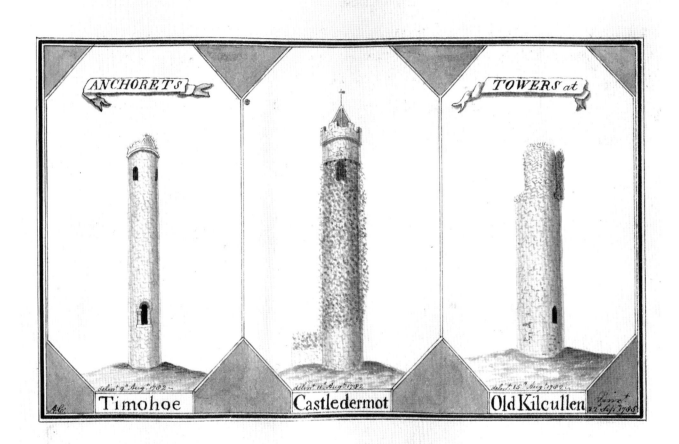

ANCHORETS TOWERS at

Timohoe   Castledermot   Old Kilcullen

OLD CASTLE, NAAS, Co. KILDARE

Page 35 of the first of the two Cooper albums of drawings in the National Library looks incomplete, having a somewhat sketchy drawing in a circle on the left, while the right-hand half remains empty. Even the solitary drawing has no caption in Cooper's own hand, but one added in pencil by a Cooper of a later generation, identifying the subject as 'Old Castle in the town of Naas'.

A peaceful market town today, Naas has lost almost all trace of its former incarnation as a medieval walled town – and a most unusual one it must have been for the number of castles it had. These were presumably the houses of well-off merchants or other denizens, and would have resembled those surviving today in places such as Dalkey, Co. Dublin and Ardglass, Co. Down – although Naas would appear to have had even more towers than they. Writing in the *Journal of the County Kildare Archaeological Society* in 1894, Thomas de Burgh listed more than a dozen; other unlocalised and unnamed examples may have increased this number, if no unintentional duplication is involved.

In his diary for 27 June 1781, Cooper noted that 'the Town of Naas is small & old-looking, having some old Castles therein & some Old houses built in that stile'. On 7 August 1782, he says that:

> near the [Gaol] wch. is an inconsiderable House just at the entrance from Dublin, stands a small square case. [Castle] of a very ancient appearance – a small distce. further on in a line with the Street & with this case. is another, much larger & of very modern appearance – between both these is another …

On 20 May 1784, Cooper mentions that 'an old case. fell down in Naas by wch. One man was killed & 2 or 3 wounded'.

Precisely which of these was the subject of Cooper's drawing must remain an open question in the absence of any identification on his part, and of any surviving remarks that might help us locate it.

Old Castle in
Town of Mads

NAUGHVAL CHURCH, Co. LAOIS

The church of Naughval (or Noughaval) may look medieval, and that is perhaps one of the reasons why Cooper sketched it. However, this is, in fact, one of the rare instances where he has turned his pen to drawing a building of his own century.

The church stands on a dominant site overlooking the town of Stradbally near the road to Portlaoise. It is a rather extraordinary structure: behind the (medieval?) tower to the right of centre in Cooper's picture stands the chancel of a church with raised interior, vaulted ceiling, and crenellated side-walls, pierced by a series of broad, rounded windows.

In his diary for 9 August 1782, Cooper describes Stradbally as 'one of the most retired & pleasant Villages I have seen in the Kingdom, with some good houses and an elegant new church' and afterwards entertains us with a brief history:

> A small distance from this town well situated on the side of a hill stands the old church of Oughvall with the walls of a modern church erected by the late Lord Sidney

which he thought to have made the parish church, but was opposed by the parishionrs, who built the aforementioned church in the town of Stradbally; consequently this lies a modern ruin. In a vault under the church is a large raised tomb of the Sidney family, wherein the late founder lies inter'd.

In his recent book *Mausolea Hibernica*, beautifully illustrated with drawings by his son Michael, Maurice Craig describes this as 'one of the most extraordinary mausolea of all'. He guessed, when it was still covered in ivy, that it was an eighteenth-century structure standing on top of the vaulted eastern limb of a ruined medieval church, now containing the enormous stone sarcophagus bearing the arms of the Cosby family. Craig notes, too, that the building was apparently designed by John Aheron, who wrote the first book on architecture ever to have been published in Ireland, *A General Treatise on Architecture in Ireland* (1754).

AC: delin.t 9.h Aug.t 1792

Emen.d 24.h Aug.t

Church of Naughval Queen's Co.t

85

KILKEA CASTLE, Co. KILDARE

Kilkea Castle, now a hotel, once claimed that it was the oldest inhabited castle in Ireland. This claim was based on the fact that there was a castle built here in 1180 by Hugh de Lacy for Walter de Riddlesford. It is a matter of conjecture as to how much, if any, of the twelfth-century castle may be incorporated in the present structure, since it may have been an earthen fortification.

In the thirteenth century, the lands of Kilkea came into the possession of the FitzGeralds, from whom the great Anglo-Irish Geraldine family took their name and – with several interruptions – they remained owners for many centuries. The castle was of strategic importance because it was located between the English Pale and the lands of the native Irish. One of the clan, Lord Edward FitzGerald, the great hero of the 1798 Rebellion, may have concealed himself in the castle for a period. Unfortunately the castle's lease-holder at the time, Thomas Reynolds, turned out to be a traitor to the cause. During the Rebellion, Government troops occupied and wrecked the castle. Other famous or infamous inhabitants of the castle included the 'Wizard Earl', who practised the 'Black Art' in the sixteenth century, various dukes of Leinster, and Co. Kildare's greatest gentleman-historian, Lord Walter FitzGerald.

Cooper's is probably the earliest-known drawing of the castle. Lord Walter reproduced it in an article he wrote about his home in the *Journal of the County Kildare Archaeological Society* in 1896. It shows a double gate giving entry to the garden, and a stairway that led to the first-floor drawing room and living room, even though the main entrance was at ground level on the other side. The castle consisted of a three-storey tower with a long, battlemented tract and a rounded tower near the gate leading to the north side. Mary Shackleton, who visited the castle in 1817, described it as having many rooms, one of which contained a tablet bearing the date 1573. At least some of the castle may well stem from this period, though Cooper maintained that it was built by John, the sixth earl of Kildare, who died in 1427.

The castle owes its present, very different, appearance to the third duke of Leinster, who made extensive alterations in 1849. He added an extra floor on top and inserted many new mullioned and transomed windows, altering the interior very considerably. Many further changes have been undertaken in the meantime.

Needless to say, a castle with such a tremendous family tradition behind it could not do without its ghost stories. These include tales of underground passages, the haunted room of the 'Wizard Earl', and the story of the old man who was built into a hole in the wall. When the hole was discovered some time early in the last century, this unhappy fellow was discovered sitting at a table with a glass – but he immediately disintegrated upon being exposed to the air.

AC. delin.t 11.th Aug.t 1782 —   Sim.t 18.th Aug.t

A SE View of Kilkea Castle Co.y Kildare

CARLOW CASTLE, Co. CARLOW

Carlow Castle had been the subject of many sketches before Cooper took his pen to it on 11 August 1782. The earliest surviving drawings of the castle are by Thomas Dineley, *c.*1680, which give details of the Elizabethan manor house that had been built inside the castle, and of which Cooper gives us some glimpses on the extreme left and in the tall chimney stack. In addition, Gabriel Beranger made copies of drawings of the castle by the landscape painter Jonathan Fisher and by Col. Charles Vallancey.

The castle itself stands on a slight but strategically important hill at the confluence of the rivers Barrow and Burren. It was built by William the Marshal, probably around 1210, though excavations by Kieran O'Conor in 1996 showed that it was preceded by a timber castle. This would have been part of a so-called ring-work, dating perhaps from around 1181, when the Normans needed to defend the adjoining crossing of the Barrow, and control shipping in this important artery linking the town with the sea at New Ross.

But when Cooper stood sketching the castle – we see him from behind in his three-cornered hat in the presence of two inquisitive onlookers – little could he imagine that most of the left-hand side of the castle as he saw it would be blown to smithereens almost thirty-two years later. By then, 1814, the castle had been leased to a physician, Dr Philip Price Middleton, who wanted to convert it into a private lunatic asylum. But, requiring larger rooms for the purpose, he decided to remove the Elizabethan interior with the aid of some blasting powder – which, on explosion, managed to remove half of the castle walls without loss of life, something which the attacks and cannons of ages had signally failed to do. The castle, as Cooper noted, was in the shape of a parallelogram with a large rounded tower at each corner – a typically Irish plan which continued to be used as late as the sixteenth century at castles such as Enniscorthy.

A.C. delin.t 11.th Aug.t 1782.   Brin.d 18.th Aug.t

A S.W. View of Carlow Castle

GRANGE CASTLE, Co. LAOIS

Not far from the River Barrow and some miles above Carlow town stood Grange Castle, a tower house which, unusually, can be dated to a particular year – thanks to Austin Cooper.

In his notes for 13 August 1782, Cooper pointed out that Grange Castle, some miles upstream from Shrule Castle, built by the Harpoles (as he called them), had an inscription over the door giving the initials RH and gb, together with the date 1588 – the year of the Spanish Armada. Lord Walter FitzGerald identified the initials as those of Robert Hartpole and his wife Grania O'Byrne. Through a drawing in Cooper's notebook, it was possible to equate the inscribed stone which he had seen at Grange Castle, bearing the same initials, with one discovered in a wall at Monksgrange, Co. Laois, around the early 1920s. This stone is now preserved in the library of the Royal Society of Antiquaries of Ireland, at 63 Merrion Square, Dublin.

Monksgrange got its name from having earlier been a grange, or out-farm, of the Cistercian abbey of Baltinglass, Co. Wicklow. In 1577, some decades after the dissolution of the monastery, this particular 'Monks' grange' was granted to Robert Hartpole, a member of an old Kent family, who was Constable of Carlow. On the very first day of that year, Hartpole, Francis Cosby of Stradbally and Shaun-a-feeka Bowen of Ballyadams had treacherously massacred some of the native gentry of counties Laois and Offaly at the Hill of Mullaghmast outside Athy. Cosby and others were subsequently taken prisoner by Rory O'Moore – described by contemporaries as Ireland's Robin Hood – but were later rescued by Hartpole, whose consequent need to be on constant guard may have led him to build the castle eleven years later. By then, however, he must have felt more secure in his territory, as the large windows and tall chimney – typical of the period – bespeak an element of domestic comfort. However, the necessity for defence is illustrated by the machicoulis beneath the parapet, from which stones could have been dropped onto unwelcome visitors trying to get through the door almost directly below.

In 1922, WG Strickland reported that the castle was incorporated in a modern dwelling house, but the *Archaeological Survey of Co. Laois* could no longer find any trace of it in 1990.

A S.W. View of Grange Castle ~ Queen's Co.

ANTIQUITIES AT OLD KILCULLEN, CO. KILDARE

Among the antiquities preserved at Old Kilcullen, you will now seek in vain for the knightly effigy on the left of Cooper's picture – not because it has been vandalised, but because it is now some seven miles away in the Church of Ireland church at Ballymore Eustace, where it has been since 1919. To it, Cooper devoted a lengthy description as follows:

> In the church yard, leaning against the S.W. corner of the church is the top of a tomb of a blackish (lime) stone, there is carved on it in Mezzo relievo, a man at full length, in armour made like fish scales, it comes over the head like a Capuchin cloke & reaches down near to the elbows & to the knees; the legs are booted & spurred; the right hand on his breast – a sword girt to his side with a remarkable narrow belt & a dog at his feet. Close to the top of his forehead is the figure of a Stag couchant (now much broken) as well as we could make it out; that shows it did belong to an Eustace.

The stag couchant, now no longer recognisable, would seem to confirm that this was a FitzEustace knight, whose effigy John Hunt dated to the early sixteenth century. Cooper's family must have exchanged drawings like this between themselves, and it is interesting to note that his cousin, Joseph Cooper Walker, reproduced this drawing in his *Historical Essay on the Dress of the Ancient and Modern Irish,* published in London in 1788.

The other two square pictures reproduced here are both from the north face of the shaft of a granite High Cross carved almost 700 years earlier than the mail-clad knight to the left of them. The lower of the two panels is the easier to identify, as it represents the Old Testament figure of Samson or, more likely, the shepherd David breaking the jaws of a lion that was about to devour the sheep visible beneath its body. The upper scene is more problematical, having been given many interpretations during the last hundred years. One of these is that it depicts a local saint, Mac Táil, laying his crozier on a prostrate person, perhaps to raise him from the dead. My own interpretation is that the panel represents the Old Testament story of Cain slaying his innocent brother Abel with an axe.

Supposed Tobe
Sir Rowland Eustace
n Gerald & Earl of
Kildare

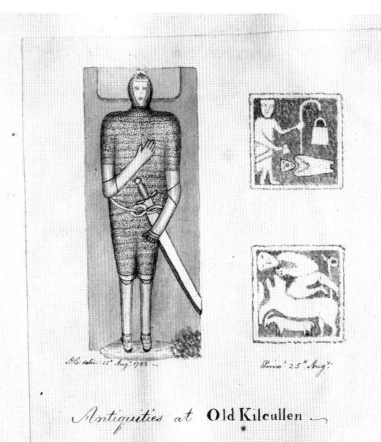

A.C. delin: 15th Aug: 1782

Pinx.t 25th Aug.t

Antiquities at **Old Kilcullen**

NEW ABBEY, KILCULLEN, Co. KILDARE

On 17 August 1782, Cooper rode out to what he described as 'a beautiful & extensive Abbey' at Kilcullen, not far from the River Liffey, and had his horse cared for while he went off to sketch. His drawing shows a long hall church, including a large ogival window with its tracery still intact. He made a plan of the structure in his diary, calling the side chapel a 'Confessional Chapel', and dividing the hall church into the choir at the eastern end, and what he mistakenly called the refectory at the western end. Cooper noted that there had been a central tower, which had fallen down around 1764.

On his plan, Cooper showed near the western end of the church the location of a double effigy, which probably represents Roland FitzEustace, baron of Portlester, and his wife Janet Bellew. It was Roland who had founded the friary for the Observantine Franciscans in 1486, and much of the fabric that Cooper saw probably dated from shortly after that time, though the three twin south windows look like an addition from the following century. The double effigy is now lying loose in the churchyard, and the surviving tomb-surrounds are built into a nearby wall.

In 1539, the priory was dissolved. By this time it consisted of 'a church, a belfry, a dormitory, a hall, two rooms and a kitchen, which are in ruins; a burial ground; an orchard; a garden and a small paddock for pasture, containing eight acres.' Its only significant lessee after that was the poet Edmund Spenser.

Cooper's sketch was made just in the nick of time for, four years later, in 1786, the church was demolished and its stones used to build a chapel which replaced it and stood until it, in its turn, was demolished in 1873. Today, only a low wall gives some indication of where the church once stood.

AC delin. 15. Aug.t 1782 —   Finis.t 18.th Aug.t

A View New Abbey near Kilcullen Co. Kildare —

MAIDEN TOWER, MORNINGTON, Co. MEATH

Cooper's two 'spectacle' views show the same monument seen from different directions, east and west respectively, as indicated by the two north compass arrows shown at the bottom of each picture. The monument is known as the Maiden Tower, and lies at the southern mouth of the River Boyne, about a mile east of Drogheda at a place called Mornington, a name said to be derived from 'Mariners' Town'.

Local tradition claims that the tower was named for Elizabeth I (1558–1603), the maiden Queen of England, but it is doubtful whether the tower dates back to her reign.

However it must have been built before 1744, when Isaac Butler visited the place and described the tower much as it is today. The battlemented parapet was probably added later in the eighteenth century.

The tower is 62ft high, and its location beside the Boyne estuary makes it likely that it was built as a navigational beacon for sailors, and probably painted white to make it more visible from a distance. This theory is supported by Cooper's outline of a sailing ship in the background. The tower, seen close by in the left-hand picture, may have served a similar purpose before the Maiden Tower was built.

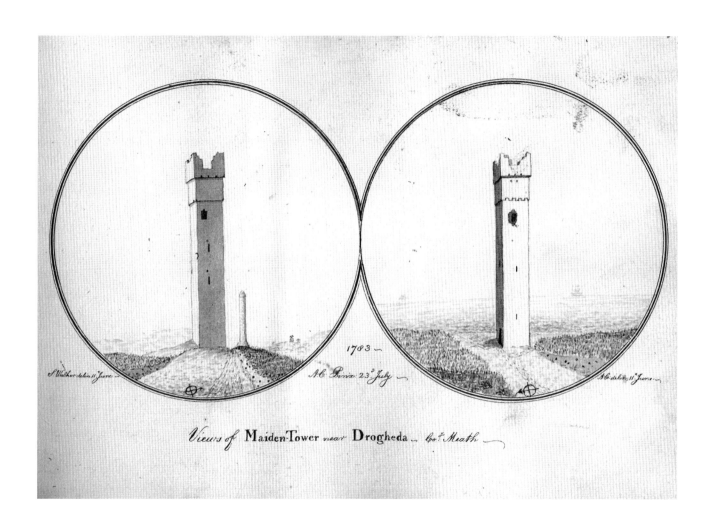

1783

Views of Maiden-Tower near Drogheda. Co.ʸ Meath

'FRANCISCAN FRIARY', DROGHEDA, Co. LOUTH

When Cooper made his sketch of what he called the Franciscan friary in Drogheda on 12 June 1783, he gave the following description of it:

> Franciscan Friery on the N. side of the river near West Gate – within the Walls ... The steeple wch. is quite entire is square & supported on a plain Gothic arch, wch. as well as all it's other parts are finished in limestone & in the same taste. There are several other pieces of the walls of this abbey remaining, but are so inveloped in the surrounding modern buildings that no idea can be formed of this particular use. The gable end at [the eastern end] is entire with a large Gothic arch entirely open wch. I suppose to have been the open from the refectory to the Choir or from the Choir to the chancel. There is a public lane through both these arches.

Things have changed comparatively little in the last 200 years, except that it is now cars and not carriages that drive underneath the arches of what has been called 'Ireland's only drive-in friary'! In *North Leinster* (1993), authors Christine Casey and Alistair Rowan described the friary's present state as 'a perfect expression of the State's lackadaisical attitude towards its historic buildings' – though its real owner is, apparently, Drogheda Corporation.

The friary is not a Franciscan friary as Cooper avers, but a priory founded for the Crutched Friars around 1206 by Urso de Swemele, which was to act as a hospital for the poor sited (*pace* Cooper) *outside*, and not *inside*, the town walls. Some of Cooper's window details do not correspond to what exists today – it is possible that they have undergone changes in the meantime, as have the buildings on either side of what is now called Abbey Lane.

A.C. delin: 12th June 1763 –   Pinx. 29th June –

A W. View of the Franciscan Friery in

Drogheda – between West Gate & the River within the Walls –

MAGDALENE TOWER, DROGHEDA, Co. LOUTH

Any visitor approaching the ancient town of Drogheda can hardly fail to see the tall Magdalene tower that stands at a height of 77ft on the top of a ridge, north of the River Boyne. Above the tall, narrow arch on the ground floor, the tower rises two further storeys, where Cooper shows windows with a central mullion forking in a curve at the top, beneath the skyline crenellations.

Access to the upper storeys was by means of a protruding stairway, shown on the right in Cooper's drawing. The tower belonged to what Cooper called the Convent of St Mary Magdalene, founded for the Dominicans by Luke Netterville, Archbishop of Armagh around 1224, and Cooper's comments about it are as follows:

> Of this abbey no traces are now remaining except the steeple, a handsome high square building wch. stands conspicuous above all the other buildings in the town near St Sunday's gate & at present is called St Sunday's Steeple; probably it had something to say to St Sunday if there be such a Saint. A particular description of this would be tedious, suffice it to say that it is perfectly Gothic – finished in limestone – & the lower part an high arch quite open. Many persons of note we are told was buried at this place, but these & all such works are totally obliterated all the ground immediately about the steeple being laid out in snug gardens.

Occasional excavations over the last forty years confirmed Cooper's remarks, as they uncovered a considerable number of burials. They also uncovered parts of the early thirteenth-century church, which was in the shape of a long rectangle, and into which the tower was built in the late fourteenth or early fifteenth century. Not even the foundations of the early church walls survive above ground and thus the tower stands as the sole reminder of what was once a rich monastery, receiving alms directly from the kings of England. One of these, Richard II, visited the priory in 1394, and had four Irish kings – including an O'Neill – submit to him.

As part of the renovation programme, Drogheda Corporation has taken out the medieval windows and replaced them correctly with limestone, but of a bright and harsh hue that seems too fresh and out of character with the grimy walls of the remainder of the tower's masonry.

AC delin: 14th June 1783.   Pinx. 30th June

A N.E: View of the Convent of St Mary Magdalen
in Drogheda; commonly called St Sunday's Steeple.

CADAVER EFFIGY, ST PETER'S, DROGHEDA, Co. LOUTH

In June 1783, Cooper visited the churchyard of St Peter's Church in Drogheda and found that:

> …in the wall are two very curious figures representg. Skeletons of a man & his wife whom it is said were eat in that manner by fishes. It is impossible to describe it, therefore must let a drawing of it answer the purpose.

Like the effigies themselves, Cooper's drawing – copied from an original by his cousin Samuel Walker, who visited the churchyard with him – is very striking, even if it fails to capture the expression in the faces of the two figures.

The effigy's purpose is to show the skeletons of a man and woman, their burial shroud open to display the cadavers decaying within, which are being preyed upon by what the antiquarian Helen Roe vividly described in 1969 as 'loathy, crawling, scaly vermin'. Recalling the old doggerel verse about how 'the worms crawl in and the worms crawl out, they go in thin and they come out stout', the intention of the effigy is therefore to remind us of our mortality. In the words of Ecclesiasticus, 'When thou diest thou shalt inherit serpents and beasts and worms'. As a translation of the inscription of a similar cadaver effigy in Kinsale, Co. Cork, puts it, 'I was as thou art and thou yet shall be / what I am now, I prithee pray for me.'

In short, it is a graphic illustration of the preoccupation with death so prevalent in the late medieval mind.

The carver has stylised the wavy lines of the respective shrouds, and has provided both cadavers with many extra ribs, the lady on the right having many more than the man. The inscription, omitted by Cooper, runs around the edge of this outside slab (8 x 5 ft), indicating that it marked the resting place of Edmund Goldyng of Peristownlaundy (now Piercetown) and Elizabeth Fleming – presumably his wife, and the daughter of the Baron of Slane. The precise identification of these persons has been a matter of some dispute, but one may have been the same Edmund Goldyng whom we know to have been alive in 1511, which would place the monument in the first third of the sixteenth century. The fact that he survived his wife (and went on to re-marry twice) might help to explain why his head is more life-like (even down to the stubble on his chin) than her more decomposed skull. The monument has now been placed upright against the interior east wall of the churchyard.

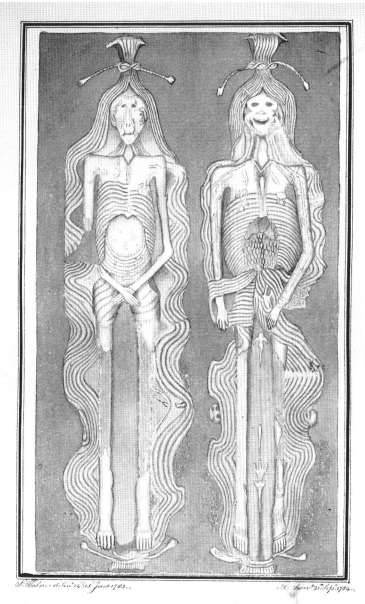

S. Walker delin. 14 & 15 June 1783.   *J.C. Scrr.t 21 Sep.t 1784.*

Part of a Tomb which lay in the Old Church of St. Peter in Drogheda; & on the rebuilding thereof was placed with others in the Church Yard Wall. See fol.g Page.

GOLDYNG AND OTHER TOMB FRAGMENTS, DROGHEDA, CO. LOUTH

While his cousin Samuel Walker was drawing the double cadaver effigy previously seen (no.44), Austin Cooper was spending part of 14 June 1783 sketching memorial stones, which are now let into the wall beside the effigy in the churchyard of St Peter's Church, Drogheda.

Only the larger of the two stones once supported the tomb of Edmund Goldyng and his wife Elizabeth Fleming. It shows two angels with curving draped bodies holding up a shield bearing what, in the often puzzling and antiquated terminology of heraldry, is described as three martlets, one above the other, in the dexter coat, and three little crosses on three cinque foils on the sinister coat. This was accompanied with an inscription – now virtually illegible – identifying the shield as that of Walter Goldyng and Elizabeth Darce (Darcy).

It is only through Cooper's notes that Lord Walter FitzGerald was able to identify the name Walter in his 1899 article on the subject in the splendidly titled *Journal of the Association for the Preservation of the Memorials of the Dead, Ireland*. In that same article, Lord Walter pointed out that the lower stone in Cooper's drawing did not belong to the Goldyng monument, but was not able to suggest for whose memorial the 6ft-long stone had been carved. It consists of a group of three arches supported by fluted Ionic columns, each bearing a shield. That in the centre shows the Resurrection of Christ as he steps out of the tomb flanked by sleeping soldiers, with a scroll above inscribed with the letters IMRI (as Cooper gives it – but perhaps, more correctly, INRI).

The adjoining shields cannot be identified; the dexter shield is the same in both as are the initials PD, while the sinister shield has different designs and the separate, uniden-tified initials AD and TW. The fluted columns would suggest a sixteenth-century date. Had it not been for Cooper's drawing, we would not have been able to read the initials, as they had all but disappeared even in Lord Walter's day a century ago.

Tomb of Edmond Spalding of Periston & Elizth Fleming daughter of the Baron of Slane

A.G. delin^t 14th June 1783. (4 f^t 2 in^s long & 2 f^t 4 in^s broad) finis^t 18th Sep^t 1784.

N:B: There are four of these in all, & only differ from each other in the Coats of Arms.

A.G. delin^t 14th June 1783. (6 feet long & 2 f^t 3 in^t broad) finis^t 1st July

In the Church Yard Wall at St Peter's **Drogheda**

See former page

Saphow tomb of Caddell family?

PRIMATE'S PALACE, TERMONFECKIN, Co. LOUTH

This 'palace', referred to as 'Termonfechan' by Austin Cooper, was named after a monastery that once stood on this site, founded by St Fechín of Fore (see no.109) in the seventh century.

But the reason why the Primate – that is, the Archbishop of Armagh – should have a palace here at all was not out of homage for this early Irish saint. It had much more to do with the religious politics of the later medieval period, when the Archbishop – usually an Englishman by birth – was surrounded by native Irish whose language he did not understand. He felt much safer when he could get away from his See at Armagh and reside at Termonfeckin, the southernmost tip of his Archdiocese, and its nearest point to the centre of English power in Dublin some thirty-five miles away.

The siege mentality of those within is reflected in the small, defendable window slits inserted in the severe-looking wall face, as seen in Cooper's drawing. In fact, Cooper criticises the inclusion of too many windows in Thomas Wright's

Louthiana of 1748, a (recently reprinted) pioneer of engraved volumes of Irish antiquities.

When Wright visited the castle, he described it as 'quite neglected and run to ruin'. Its last inhabitant had been the Irish scholar Archbishop James Ussher, one of whose main claims to fame was to have teased out from the Bible that this world was created in the year 4004 BC.

By 1792, when Daniel Grose visited the castle, it was in a much more ruinous state than when Wright sketched it forty-four years earlier. Grose shows massive holes in the east and west walls, which must inevitably have led to the collapse of the castle, so complete that not a trace of it exists today. Also gone is the rounded turret a few yards to the south, which Cooper supposed 'to have belonged to some of its external improvements'. The eastern view suggests that the castle was located on the southern bank of the river, to the west of the bridge – probably for security reasons.

A:C: delin. 12ᵗʰ June 1783 ~   Pinx. 3ᵈ July

An E; View of the Primate's Palace at Termon-fechan co. Louth ~

TERMONFECKIN CASTLE, Co. LOUTH

While Austin Cooper was occupied in sketching the Primate's Palace at Termonfeckin on 12 June 1783, his cousin Samuel Walker – who must have been accompanying him on this trip – went a few hundred yards west towards the sea to draw a much smaller tower house. Cooper has labelled this 'Termonfechan Castle', to differentiate it from the palace. Unlike the larger and more brooding palace, however, the castle survives. Cooper says of it that:

> … on a hill on the opposite side of this village stands a small old Case. [Castle] wch. the people there say belonged to the Clergyman of the Parish and is still in possn. of the Incumbent, but the use he makes of it is to serve as a 'Granary to collect his Tythes'.

The three-storey tower house, a national monument, has undergone many changes over the years and is lacking the projecting towers that it must have had at two of its corners.

The most interesting feature of this tower is the corbelled vault of the second floor, a superb piece of masonry. This vault was built in the same technique that was used in the burial chamber at Newgrange some 4500 years earlier, but its thinner, flatter slabs cover a much wider area. It seems all the more remarkable when viewed today from the ground floor, but we ought not to forget that there were intermediate floors, long since disintegrated, which would have detracted from its visual splendour.

The castle may have been built for some religious or lay dependant of the Archbishop of Armagh, or even by a merchant trading in the shadow of his palace. However, we do not even know which family built it, though the Dowdalls of Newtown, not far away, have been mentioned more than once in this connection. The lower building shown by Cooper has now vanished, but otherwise there has been little change in the castle, for better or for worse, in the meantime.

S. Walker delin. 12.th June 1783.   M. Pinx. 22.d July 1783.

A NE: View of Termon-fechan Castle, Co. Louth.

DULEEK CHURCH, Co. MEATH

The name of the village of Duleek in Co. Meath is derived from the Old Irish word, *damhliag,* meaning a stone oratory. Legend suggests that this was the location of Ireland's oldest stone church, built in the fifth or sixth century by St Cianán, who is alleged to have been one of the first bishops in Ireland, ordained by St Patrick himself.

We can discount the notion that this early church is the one Cooper illustrated in his sketch of 13 June 1783. Cooper's church is probably a thousand years younger, and a carved head-capital preserved in the church shows that there was at least one intermediate church built there in the twelfth century. The massive tower seen in the background is in the style of the fifteenth century, and is remarkable because it was built up against (and partly enclosed) an old Irish Round Tower which has since disintegrated, leaving only its negative trace in the north wall of the tower. Beneath the three-light east window seen here is a dated inscription as follows:

This window was made by Sirr
Johne Bellewe Knight and Dame
Ismay Nugent his wife in the
year of the Lord 1587

Within the church is buried another John Bellewe who, as the inscription states, 'was shot in the belly in Oughrim fight the first of July 1691' – and Duleek had featured earlier in the same campaign when King William slept there after his victory on the River Boyne.

The building shown on the right was replaced by a Church of Ireland parish church, which was built in 1816 and which, like its predecessor, has since been boarded up. On the other side of it is a small High Cross. This was 'adorned with some curious figures, wch. time wod. not permit me to copy', according to Cooper who, in fact, like most of his contemporaries, showed little interest in High Crosses.

A.C. delin. 13th June —   Pinxt. 4th July 1783 —

A S.E. View of Duleek Church Co.y Meath

EFFIGY IN THE CHURCH AT DULEEK, Co. MEATH

Writing about the church in Duleek, Co. Meath, in his diary of 13 June 1783, Austin Cooper says that:

Under the E. window of an old tomb are the Effs. of a mitred abbot or Bishop with a Crozier in his left hand, & on the right side a coat of arms blank with a Mermaid for a Crest. At his feet had been an inscripn. now worn off, but from the Crest I suppose his name to have been St Laurence.

The effigy is now placed on its side in the same arcade, and close to the window mentioned by Cooper. It is not, however, of a member of the St Laurence family, as Cooper supposed, but of a Dr James Cusack.

Dr Cusack 'was related to many of the Catholic nobility of the Pale', according to Cogan's *History of the Diocese of Meath* (1870), and a 'man of great merit for his learning and prudence and earnestness' in the words of his college contemporary, the canonised primate, Oliver Plunket. Dr Cusack was made coadjutor of Meath in 1678 and died as bishop a decade later, after James II of England had ascended the throne, and induced in Ireland the hope of more liberal times for his Catholic subjects.

This was also a period when there was a flowering of local monumental sculpture, as studied by the archaeologist Heather King, and this is a good product of the Meath school. The stone from which it is carved is more than 7ft long and shows the bishop in his full canonicals – including a stepped mitre – carved in relief in a pointed niche. The crozier with outward-facing crook, which he holds in his left hand, stands out from the surface of the stone, and his coat of arms – better preserved then than it is today – is shown on the other side of his head.

What is so unusual about this monument is that the other side bears a rough-out of a better-preserved episcopal effigy (presumably also Dr Cusack) facing the opposite way round. It is much smaller in scale and was probably face down on the ground in the eighteenth century, so that Cooper may never have seen it. Though Cooper may have placed the effigy on its side to maximise the space on his page, it is fortunate that the tombstone is currently displayed in exactly the same way today, as it gives us the advantage of being able to see both the finished and the unfinished sides.

Ab: delin: 13th June 1745 —   Pinx: 5 July —

A Tomb in the Church of **Duleck** – Co: Meath –

FACES OF THE CROSS AT DULEEK, CO. MEATH

The county of Meath is fortunate in having had a number of wealthy patrons who put up commemorative or wayside crosses from the fifteenth to the seventeenth centuries.

One of the more remarkable of these patrons was Dame Jennet Dowdall, who would have been forgotten by history had she not erected four crosses – two for each of her two husbands. Her second husband was Oliver Plunket, whom she married after the death of her first, William Bathe, in Dublin, in 1599. Both of the crosses she erected in memory of Bathe are located in or near the town of Duleek – one outside the village, on the roadside at Annesbrooke, the other, here illustrated, on a platform on one of the village greens in the town itself.

Cooper's drawing shows left and right the two broad faces of the cross – or what is left of them, as the lower part of the shaft and the head of the cross are missing and were obviously already so in Cooper's day. Each side of the collar on top bears an angel holding up implements of the Passion, identified by Heather King as the whipping post, scourges and lantern on the left, and a heart with the Crown of Thorns and pincers on the right. On what Cooper gives as the south side (now the west face), he shows the coat of arms of Bathe and Dowdall impaled, but omitting most of the carved detail and with the initials and family names of the couple displayed above. Under the letters IHS beneath the coat of arms is a long inscription in high relief, which Cooper copied very carefully, as he did the inscriptions above the names of Saints Peter, Patrick and Cianán on his north side (now the east face). How the original artist, Cooper's cousin Samuel Walker, managed to confuse the words Barnabe and Cianán (or Keenane as it was originally carved), we shall never know.

The upper shaft fragment, as drawn in the illustration opposite, shows two faces. One face shows what looks like the lower part of a scene representing Christ being taken down from the cross, above a hooded figure. The other face shows the lower part of a Crucifixion scene, above what looks like an Ecce Homo. These are valuable records, as the face of the upper fragment has been re-cut, destroying some of the details shown here.

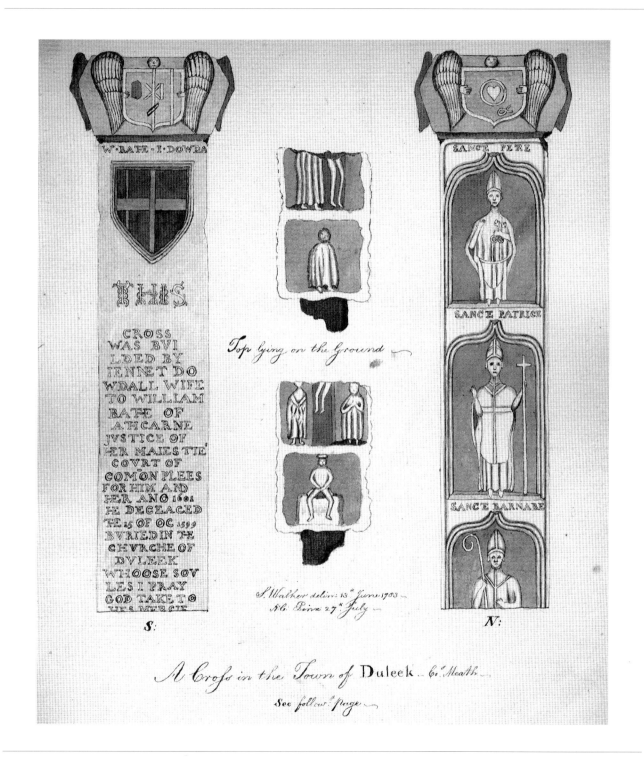

W·BATE · I · DOWDA

THIS
CROSS
WAS BVI
LDED BY
IENNET DO
WDALL WIFE
TO WILLIAM
BATE OF
ATHCARNE
IVSTICE OF
HER MAIESTIE
COVRT OF
COMON PLEES
FOR HIM AND
HER ANO 1601
HE DECEACED
TE 15 OF OC 1599
BVRIED IN TE
CHVRCHE OF
DVLEEK
WHOOSE SOV
LES I PRAY
GOD TAKE TO
TES MERCIE

S:

Top lying on the Ground

S. Walker delin: 13th June 1783
N G. Pinx 27th July

SANCE PETRE

SANCE PATRICE

SANCE BARNABE

N:

A Cross in the Town of Duleek. C. Meath

See follow.g page

SIDES OF THE CROSS AT DULEEK, CO. MEATH

Most of this illustration is taken up with the narrow sides of the cross erected at Duleek in 1601 by Dame Jennet Dowdall in memory of her deceased husband, William Bathe. As on the faces of the cross reproduced on the previous page (no.50), we have the items associated with Christ's Passion held by winged angels on the collar – Pilate, with soldier's dice and the rope on the left side, and the towel of Veronica bearing Christ's face on the right.

The saints depicted on the left are Andrew, Catherine (*not* Hatre as Cooper has written here) and Stephen (Steven), the first martyr. St Mary Magdalene, and the Apostles James and Thomas are on the right. The carvings on the two sides of the upper part of the shaft are unusual: one is showing an apparently naked figure with his foot on an animal – St George and the Dragon; while the other shows a second figure standing over another dragon – perhaps the Archangel Michael.

More intriguing is the insertion on this page of a coat of arms and the initials IB and IN from a stone in the bridge of Bellewstown. I have been unable to find this inscribed stone, so this is perhaps our only record of it. The initials are those of the couple we have already encountered as having commissioned the east window in the church at Duleek (no.48) namely John(e) Bellew(e) and his wife Dame Ismay Nugent, whose initials and an almost identical coat of arms are found on a plaque on the bridge at Ballinacor, Co. Westmeath, showing that the pair must have made quite a habit of building bridges.

S·ANDRE

S·HATRE

S·STEVEN

Top
as before

IB   IN

S·Walter
delin 13 June
1788

J. C. Prince
27 July
1788

Inscription on the Bridge of
Bellewstown

E:

S·M·MAGD

S·IACOBE

S·THOM

W:

The other sides of the Cross in Duleek
See former page

MOUNT at DULEEK, Co. Meath

In his diary for 13 June 1783, in connection with a visit to the Co. Meath town of Duleek, Austin Cooper noted that:

> At the N.side of this town stands a large Danish Mount, wch. being composed of good gravel is very much cut away & will in a short time be all taken away.

How right he was. The inroads he describes and illustrates have taken their toll to such an extent that not a trace remains of this motte.

The Danes (that is, the Vikings) have been made responsible for many things in this country – Danes' Forts or ringforts, among others – but it was a later invasion of ultimately Nordic relations, in the form of the Normans, who would have built this motte. It was almost certainly the great Norman baron, Hugh de Lacy, who raised it, for he established a manor here, probably in the 1170s. Around 1180 he granted the local parochial church of St Cianán to the Augustinian priory of Llanthony Secunda in Gloucestershire, whose friars built a grange, or farmhouse, for their new estate at Duleek.

We tend to think of destruction of earthworks as a regrettable modern phenomenon. This illustration reminds us, sadly, that the habit has been going on for centuries. In this instance, if it had not been for Cooper's cousin, Samuel, drawing this motte, we might never have known what it looked like.

S. Walker delin.

13ᵗʰ June 1783

A.C. Pinxᵗ.

24ᵗʰ July 1783

A W: View of the Mount at Duleek, Coᵗ Meath

SOUTH-EAST VIEW OF BARBERSTOWN CASTLE, CO. KILDARE

Barberstown Castle stands beside a crossroads, where routes from Celbridge, Maynooth, Clane and Straffan converge. When Cooper visited it one late September day in 1783, he would have been surrounded by trees gradually turning to their russet autumn hue. Eight years later, in March 1791, Cooper wrote in his diary, 'rode to J. Atkinson's at Barberstown'. This Mr Atkinson may well have been Cooper's host on his visit in 1783, and he is seen here, exercising his dog in a raised garden behind the outer wall, while Cooper busies himself with his drawing pad at the bottom of the picture.

The modern tarmac avenue to the castle follows the same path as the eighteenth-century pattern of field-fencing.

Today, the gate on the left is kept open for the guests of what is now a luxury hotel. The central tower's stone-vaulted ground floor now functions as a 'medieval' restaurant, its walls festooned with animal heads shot and stuffed in more recent centuries. The bedrooms above offer vastly more comfort than any medieval guest would ever have enjoyed.

The house on the right had a single extraordinarily tall chimney, but its square windows suggest a date no earlier than the eighteenth century. Yet, this house has disappeared, while the castle remains, having been replaced at various stages up until the 1830s, when the present wing to the north of the castle achieved its final form.

A S.E. View of Barberstown Castle Co. Kildare

AC: delin: 29.ᵗʰ Sept. 1783   Sinx: 2.ᵈ Oct.ᵗ

WEST VIEW OF BARBERSTOWN CASTLE, Co. KILDARE

The gate at the end of the avenue, seen closed in the previous illustration (no.53), led into a courtyard. This had another entrance from outside, seen in the drawing opposite, which Cooper executed on the same visit. Though the low buildings surrounding this courtyard today have replaced those shown by Cooper, they still give the same atmosphere of an enclosed and comfortable farmyard, where hotel guests now park their cars.

The name Barberstown derives from the Barby family, who owned the area in the late thirteenth century. However, the castle changed hands so many times during the later medieval period that we do not know exactly which family was involved in building it.

It is a typical small tower house, of a kind found in a thousand and more examples throughout the Irish country-side. The great majority of these houses were erected as family homes during the fifteenth and sixteenth centuries and Barberstown is probably no exception. It seems to have been considered a prize worth having. According to legend, one inhabitant was so unwilling to part with it, that he had himself buried in the tower to retain possession by ruse. He did this, so the story went, so that his family would not have to hand over the castle on his death, because the lease stipulated that it would come to an end when he was 'put underground'!

A subsequent owner, in the eighteenth century, was Bartholomew Van Homrigh, whose daughter was Vanessa, immortalised by Jonathan Swift. Still more recently, it was owned by another well-known name, the singer-songwriter Eric Clapton. In between, the house was owned by the Barton family, who completed the main part of the castle around the 1830s, and whose name adorns many bottles of good French wine to this day. It is appropriate, therefore, that the present owners, Kenneth and Catherine Healy, should have a Château Langoa Barton on the wine-list of what is now a very exclusive country-house hotel.

A W: View of Barberstown Castle — Co: Kildare

MALLOW CASTLE, Co. CORK

The rather skeletal trees in the picture opposite are evidence that it was in the winter that Austin Cooper made his sketch of Mallow Castle, which is very much in the centre of the north Cork town of the same name.

The land the castle stands on was formerly O'Keeffe territory, before coming into the hands of the Norman Roches. The Desmond branch of the FitzGerald family then acquired the area. However, Elizabeth I took the land from them, and granted the castle and manor of Mallow to the Lord-President of Munster, Sir Thomas Norreys, in 1584. Whatever castle was there at that time was later replaced by the existing structure, which is better described as a manor than a castle, since its plentiful windows indicate a peaceful rather than a military use – although provision was still made for the protection of musketeers firing from the castle.

It is the castle's main front, looking north-west, that Cooper chooses to show here. The façade, once plastered all over, is flanked at each end by an angular tower, and access was gained through the far side of the central tower, which is three storeys high. The windows were better preserved in Cooper's day and it is, presumably, only by mistake that he omitted the two three-light examples at first-floor level between the central polygonal tower and the flanking turret on the left. The unexpectedly large arch in the side-wall may have been associated with a fire-place in a kitchen building, which may have been added on secondarily to the south-west gable of the castle, and which has long since disappeared.

The castle, so very English in character, may date from around 1610, the period when Norrey's only daughter Elizabeth – doubtless named after the queen whose god-child she was – married Sir John Jephson, whose family continued to own the castle until recently. But it has long been uninhabited – probably since the 1640s, when it must have suffered in successive sieges, firstly by the Confederate forces under Viscount Mountgarret in 1642, then by Lord Castlehaven in 1645, and finally by the Parliamentarians under Lord Inchiquin in 1646.

A S.W: View of Mallow Castle, Co: Cork.

MOONE CHURCH, Co. KILDARE

St Colmcille, or Columba, is traditionally associated with Moone, where the presence of two ninth-century High Crosses certainly argues in favour of the existence of an early monastery – and one of these even gives a hint of a connection with the Columban foundation at Kells. But much of the church illustrated by Cooper comes from a later period when Henry of London, one of the first English archbishops of Dublin, granted the church of Moone Columbkill, with its appended chapels, to the Cathedral of St Patrick in Dublin in 1225.

A part of that church at the eastern end of the present structure (the far gable in Cooper's drawing) has been revealed to be pre-Norman in date, through an examination and excavation carried out recently by Miriam Clyne. But the remainder of the church as seen in the drawing is no earlier than the thirteenth century, and some of it – particularly the middle wall with small belfry on top – may be later still in date, for the 110ft-long church was shortened, perhaps due to a dwindling congregation. The hall-like nature of the church could lend support to a local tradition that the Franciscans had a house at Moone, but no documentary evidence exists to confirm the claim. Nevertheless, it is quite likely that some kind of monastic community existed at Moone in the later medieval period.

The unusual tall square tower behind the church is also late medieval. From the rubble of the collapse or demolition of this tower, three carved fragments were found that went to make up the famous High Cross at Moone. For protection against the weather, the cross has recently been brought inside the walls of the ruined church, which, it is hoped, will be re-roofed soon. It is displayed there beside another, much more fragmentary, cross, which has a hole at the centre of its head. This second cross has artistic links with yet another cross at Finglas in Co. Dublin, whence a zeal to reform the Irish church emanated at the end of the eighth century – shortly before both crosses at Moone were carved.

A. delin.^t March 1784.

Jam.^s G. March.

A N.W. View of the Church of Moon ∼ Co. Kildare

ROSCREA ROUND TOWER, Co. TIPPERARY

Austin Cooper's first album of drawings in the National Library contains two separate drawings of the Round Tower at Roscrea: the one here depicted (which is no.58 in the album), and no.62 in this volume (which is no.63 in the album). The latter was entirely his own work, sketched on the spot on 16 June 1784, and worked up on 20 July. But the former is probably Cooper's copy of a sketch by the fine painter and watercolourist, John James Barralet (1747–1815).

Earlier in 1784, on 10 April, Cooper had copied into his album this drawing and, as we can see from the inscription beneath the bottom left of the tower plinth, credited it to 'JJ Bt' – or John James Barralet.

Barralet had trained in the Dublin Society Schools before going to London in 1770. He then returned to teach at his alma mater in 1779 – and it was probably around this time that he executed his drawing of the Round Tower at Roscrea. This might well have been at the request of the noted antiquarian William Burton (later Conyngham), who commissioned Barralet to accompany Gabriel Beranger on a tour of Wexford in 1779 to sketch antiquities.

Not having obtained a permanent post as teacher with the Dublin Society, Barralet sailed for America in 1795. There he executed some of his best-known works, associated with the emerging post-colonial nation, as outlined by Anne Crookshank and the Knight of Glin in their splendid volume *The Watercolours of Ireland* (1994). Barralet often enlivened his compositions with trees and figures, as well as horses and carriages, but the only such element to be seen here is the man standing on the bottom right. This figure seems so pygmy-sized that one wonders if he were not an addition by Cooper, who often shows himself with a three-cornered hat, as worn by the small figure.

It should be said that architecture was not one of Barralet's specialities, and he has stylised the irregular masonry of the tower into regimented rows of ashlar masonry, which make it look more like a Classical campanile than the irregularly coursed masonry of an old Irish monastic Round Tower.

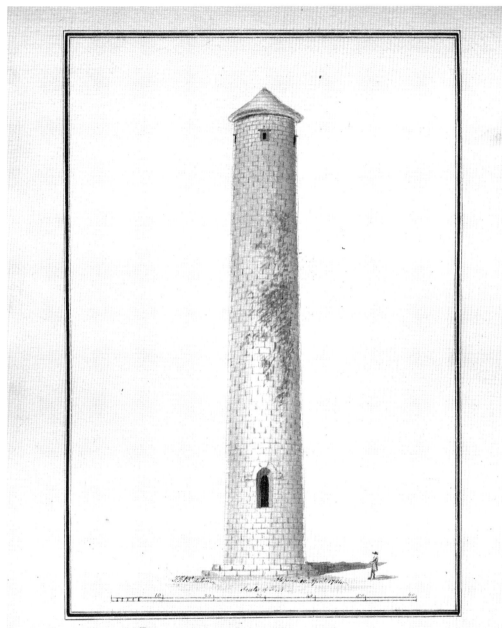

Round Tower at **Roscrea** *Co. Tipperary*

(See page 63)

BURNTCOURT CASTLE, Co. TIPPERARY, FROM THE RIVER

Forty years separate the execution of Anthony Chearnley's original drawing of Burntcourt Castle in Co. Tipperary from the copy illustrated opposite, which was made by Austin Cooper in 1784. Exactly the same illustration was engraved in 1792 for the second volume of Grose's *Antiquities of Ireland* – but in a rectangular form, showing that it was Cooper who added the panoramic television-screen effect.

Cooper's drawing shows the south-eastern side of the ruined 'manor of Everard's Castle', as it was called when Charles I of England granted the ground it stands on, and much more, to Sir Richard Everard. Everard had had to resign his judgeship in the previous reign of James I because he was a Catholic. Historical sources would agree with the caption to the picture, which states that Everard built the castle in 1641. In the words of the castle expert, HG Leask, it was 'perhaps the most perfect, as also the latest, of a type of towered and gabled house common in the South of Ireland'.

In plan, the castle has a square tower at each corner of a central oblong block and, as well as a number of tall chimneys, it had a total of twenty-six gables. Unlike the narrow defensive slits of medieval tower houses, Burntcourt has large, four-part windows, all slightly higher off the ground than expected, just in case an attack came – which it did.

Here, once again, the caption would seem to be right, as Cromwell wrote to the English Parliament at the end of January 1650 to the effect that he 'marched to a strong house called Clogheen belonging to Sir Richard Everard' who, he states, was a member of the Supreme Court, appointed by the Confederation of Kilkenny in 1646. Everard retreated and got as far as Limerick where he was hanged by Ireton the following year. Tradition claims that it was Everard himself or his wife who set fire to the castle, thereby giving it its name (now shared with the village that lies beside it, close to the Mitchelstown–Cahir road). A local rhyme said of it that 'it was seven years in building, seven years living in it, and fifteen days it was burning'.

The mysterious game being played in the left foreground draws attention away from the sad and gaunt ruins. There are three unevenly spaced pairs of uprights, with a net spanned between each pair. One man (looking like an ice hockey player from the back) seems to be defending his 'wicket' against a 'bowler' with one knee on the ground. A bystander looks on, as well as some interested and expectant canines. With the trees showing signs of winter, this painting seems to echo distantly Dutch landscape painting of the seventeenth century.

Anthony Chearnley delin.t 1744

M.r Pins.t 15.t April 1784

A S.E: Prospect of **Burntcourt** from the River. C.y Tipperary

This strong Castle was built about the time of the troubles in 1641 by Sir Richard Everard an Irish Knight. It was afterwards surrendered to **Cromwel** and mention is made of it in his life where he went over the river **Suir** & took in the strong Castle of **Cloghern** (**Burntcourt**). It was soon after burnt by the Irish to prevent it's being enjoyed by a Protestant Adventurer.

NORTH-WEST PROSPECT OF BURNTCOURT CASTLE, CO. TIPPERARY

Again using his TV panoramic (or, should we say, rear-view mirror) effect, Cooper shows us Burntcourt Castle from another angle, as drawn forty years earlier by Anthony Chearnley, an artist whose house (now vanished) appears in the right-hand side of the picture.

Grose's *Antiquities of Ireland*, which also reproduces an engraving of this scene, describes Chearnley as a man who 'deserves to be remembered for cultivating the art of design when few pursued it' – perhaps a reference to his style of gardening, as seen in the foreground. Grose also noted that Chearnley was one of the earliest collectors of antiquarian drawings in Ireland.

Chearnley painted a very competent picture of the town of Kinsale and it is his quality draughtsmanship that raises Cooper's standard to above the usual. Interestingly, while the caption to Cooper's copy of 1784 states that the original was

in the possession of the Rev. Mr Archdall (author of the *Monasticon Hibernicum* of 1786), it had, according to Grose's *Antiquities*, joined the collection of the Right Hon. William (Burton) Conyngham sometime during the following decade.

This interesting composition gives us good details of the castle windows and gables, and also shows the corbels above the first-floor windows, which must have borne defensive timber galleries along the whole front of the central block. It is also interesting to note how the decorative garden – or at least the visible part of it – is placed outside a tall wall, which surrounds the whole castle complex, and which survives in part, though not on the side shown here. The small conical shrubs lining the avenue leading up to the entrance gate provide an attractive contrast to the rows of tall trees seen in the background here, and on the right in the previous picture.

Anthony Chearnley delin.t 1744 —

A.C. Pinx.t 21.st April 1784 —

A N:W Prospect of the Castle of **Burntcourt** & part of the Author's Dwelling House —

This & the foregoing View of this extensive Building are copied from the Original in the possession of the —
Rev.d M.r Archdall —

FIRE-HOUSE, Kildare

St Brigid is generally credited with having founded a double monastery at Kildare around the sixth century – one for monks and one for nuns. Her seventh-century biographer, Cogitosus, describes a great wooden church in which she and Bishop Conlaed were buried side by side in spectacular sarcophagi.

St Brigid and her nuns tended a famous fire that the Welsh historian, Giraldus Cambrensis, put at the top of the list of miracles associated with her:

> First there is the inextinguishable fire; not because it cannot be put out but because the nuns and holy women supply materials to the fire so carefully and accurately that it has remained without being quenched ever since the time of the holy virgin through such a lapse of years. In the saint's time there were here twenty nuns, she being the twentieth. Never since has the number increased. And when each one in her turn watches the fire for a night, when the twentieth night comes, the nun, having laid on it the wood, says: 'Brigit, take care of your fire.' And the wood is found to be consumed in the morning, and the fire still lighting. And though so vast a quantity of wood hath been in such a length of time consumed in it, yet the ashes have never increased.

Richard Stanihurst, who visited Kildare in the sixteenth century specifically to see it, described the fire-house as 'a monument lyke a vaute', though there was nothing like a vault surviving when Cooper visited Kildare in 1784. He gave the measurements as 30ft x 15ft, sketched one gable with a gaping hole and an even more ruinous one at the other end.

Today, the remains are even more meagre, all that is visible today being a roughly square wall (very different from Cooper's proportions!) little more than a foot high, located to the north of the nave of the cathedral that dominates the town.

Henry of London, the English Archbishop of Dublin from 1223 to 1228, is said to have extinguished the fire – after the monastery itself had ceased to function, though there is reason to suspect that it kept burning until the end of the medieval period. Some say it was extinguished because the ritual smacked of the Vestal Virgins of Ancient Rome, or other pagan practices, but the former existence of another such fire-house at the Cathedral at Cloyne in Co. Cork suggests that there was definitely something Christian about keeping this particular flame alight.

Ab. delin. 15 June 1784

Brioss. 1st July

The Fire-House of the Nuns of St Brigid at Kildare.

GREY ABBEY, KILDARE

Beside the road heading south-westwards from Kildare town towards Nurney and Athy is a decaying, ivied building, which is all that survives of the Franciscan friary commonly known as the Grey Abbey.

The Grey Abbey was founded around 1260, either by Gerald FitzMaurice or William de Vesci, depending on the source used. The details of the church as shown by Cooper in his drawing of 1784 could be seen to support such a date, particularly the narrow, lancet windows in the north wall, and the buttresses in between them and on the corner of the east gable. But the single, broad, east window, with its switch-line tracery, looks as if it may have been a fifteenth-century altera-tion. The buttresses, sadly, no longer do their work effectively and the side walls might well have collapsed long ago if modern wooden buttresses had not been put up to support them. Even then, the building is described as dangerous. We are fortunate that Cooper executed this drawing when he did,

as he records features – such as the switch-line tracery of the east window and the upper part of the west gable – that have now disappeared.

Among the friars who busied themselves around the church in the late medieval period was one Brother Michael of Kildare, a satirical poet who turned his pen against the secular clergy. He also lambasted the Co. Wexford town of New Ross, when he described how its walls had had to be built to prevent the 'greedy snatching of the Irish enemies'!

The friary was rich and important enough to attract within its walls the mortal remains of no fewer than ten earls of Kildare. When the friary came to be dissolved at the Refor-mation, the church had a tower and good parts of a cloister which managed to survive a fire kindled subsequently so as to prevent the English king getting his hands on the buildings – but neither belfry nor cloister survive today.

A.C:delin. 15.th June 1784 —   Print. 10.th July —.

A N:E: View of Grey Abbey near Kildare

ROUND TOWERS AT ROSCREA, CO. TIPPERARY (A), AND KILKENNY (B)

A few pages back (no.57) we saw John James Barralet putting a neat conical top on the Round Tower at Roscrea. Here Cooper shows the structure without the cap, but with some foliage. A maximum of only five years separates the two drawings – and it is unlikely that it was in that short space of time that the conical cap fell in. So, which drawing is accurate? Is there a certain amount of artistic reconstruction in Barralet's version?

Cooper's diary sheds no light on the conundrum. We do know, however that, at some point, the top of the tower was lopped off and denuded of its uppermost set of windows, which are shown in Barralet's drawing (but not in Cooper's). This happened allegedly after the tower had been used by a sniper to fire pot-shots at the nearby castle across the roof-tops of the town.

The small house we can see beside the tower was later replaced by a three-storey stone mill-building, accompanied by a mill-pond, which lapped against the 10ft-deep foundations of the tower. Later still a disfiguring garage was built next to the tower but, thanks to the initiative of Dr George Cunningham and the Roscrea Heritage Society, it has been demolished, and the tower stands alone in isolated splendour.

The tower's round-headed doorway looks across to the fine Romanesque gable of the twelfth-century church dedicated to St Cronan (no.63), the seventh-century founder of the monastery in Roscrea of which the tower is the oldest surviving witness.

In contrast, the doorway of the Round Tower in Kilkenny turns its back on the accompanying church – the great Gothic Cathedral of St Canice overlooking the 'marble city' on the River Nore. As is often the case, Cooper extracts the monument from its background, and leaves out all trace of the Cathedral, which we would have been able to see behind it. On top there is now a metal cage – rather unsightly but very necessary for those who want to climb to the top of one of the very few Round Towers in Ireland where that is possible.

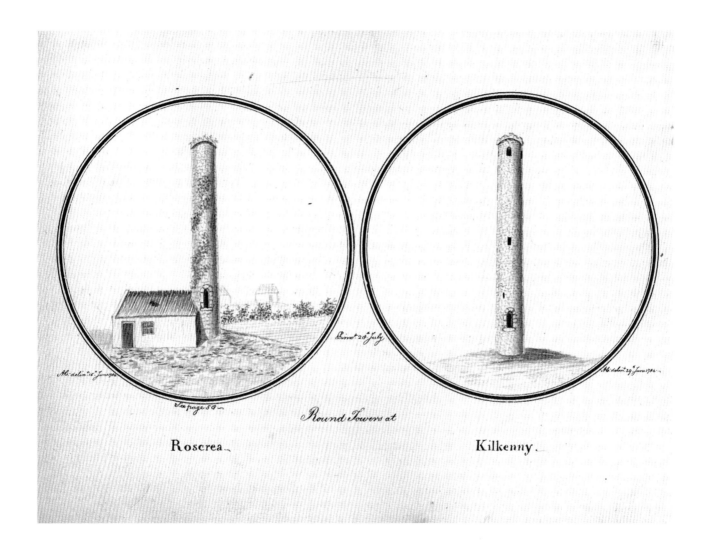

Round Towers at

Roscrea.   Kilkenny.

ST CRONAN'S CHURCH, ROSCREA, Co. TIPPERARY

Thank heavens for the Roscrea by-pass, for it means that now far fewer juggernauts and less traffic rumble through the town, causing deterioration to the façade of St Cronan's church, which has scarcely the width of a footpath between itself and the street.

What we see here is the west gable of the church. Its flanking *antae* are projecting towards us at the corner, and there is a symmetrical composition consisting of a central round-headed doorway, accompanied on each side by a double-blind arcade, all of which have tangent gables above them. The doorway's decoration is schematised by Cooper, and that of the arcades is omitted altogether. However, Cooper did include the figure of an ecclesiastic between two rosettes in the tangent gable above the doorway. This is usually identified – though not with any certainty – as St Cronan himself, the local saint to whom the church was dedicated. The level of the ground in front of the church seems to be higher here than it is today.

After Cormac's Chapel in Cashel, this church – along with the Romanesque part of Ardfert Cathedral in Kerry – is one of the main witnesses to the pioneering role that the province of Munster played in the dissemination, throughout twelfth-century Ireland, of the Romanesque style of architecture. The date of St Cronan's is uncertain, but one of the most likely candidates for its builder is Isaac O Cuanain (died 1161), the only bishop of Roscrea known from the twelfth century.

Today, only the façade of the church remains, the rest of it having been demolished in the 1820s – the gable was left standing, doubtless, because of its architectural merit. But it is a pity that Austin Cooper gave us just a straight frontal view, for had he given us a view partially from the side we would know better whether the church was cruciform or not. Now only an archaeological excavation could tell.

JC delin.t 15 Juni
1784

Painxt 6.t July

W.t End of **Roscrea Church**, Co.t Tipperary

ROSCREA CASTLE, Co. TIPPERARY

The Castle of Roscrea is a large square building and very high, of 3 Stories – the first or ground Storey was formed by timber work, the second is very lofty and arched over and in good order – the upper was formed by the roof now gone. There is a flight of steps leading to the Top and to towers at each angle. The high Chimnies appear to be of more modern date than the lower part as they are those of what I call castellated Houses which came into use about Charles 1st time, at which period I conclude from this circumstance it was inhabited.

Thus wrote Austin Cooper in his diary of 2 May 1812, and things haven't changed much since then. He continues by describing the curtain walls attached to the castle, which are punctuated by three large bastions; one bears the Duke of Ormond's coat of arms in stucco.

Cooper presumed that the manor tower was later than two of the bastions, which he thought were built in 1220. He also mentions the early eighteenth-century Damer House, which stands in the middle of the castle complex, and which is now used as a show-house and museum by the Roscrea Heritage Society. Where the long wall looks onto the street in the foreground of Cooper's picture, a drawbridge and portcullis has now been installed to great effect by Dúchas – Ireland's Heritage Service.

The usually accepted date for the castle is around the 1280s, but it may stand on the site of an earlier motte and bailey. The whole complex went through much turbulence and changes of ownership in the 1640s and 1650s, but it has survived all onslaughts to remain Roscrea's most dominant landmark, lording it over the town to this day.

AC: delin 15 June 1794   Pinxt 11th July

A N.E: View of Roscrea Castle. Co Tipperary.

143

NENAGH CASTLE, Co. TIPPERARY

Anyone approaching the town of Nenagh today cannot fail to be impressed by the tall, crenellated round bastion, which broods over the town like an *eminence grise*. But, equally, they may be either disappointed that it does not look taller in Cooper's drawing opposite, or surprised that it seems to have risen in stature since Cooper's day – which, in fact, it has.

The local historian, Dermot F Gleeson, tells of how his uncle, a priest, was sent to America to raise funds for the building of a church – and, having failed to collect enough cash, stayed there. However, the £600 he *had* gathered was put to good local use by the bishop, who used it to add 25ft to the top of the tower, including the crenellations and the chaplet of tall windows beneath.

The tower itself was the strong citadel of a castle erected in the first decades of the thirteenth century by Theobald Walter, on lands given to him by Henry II. This castle was to become the main focus of Anglo-Norman settlement in North Tipperary. The tower was one of three spaced along the rounded curtain wall of an enclosure, to which access was gained through a gateway, flanked by two smaller round towers. Later in the century, a large rectangular building – seen here, on the right – was added, so that its first floor could act as a hall for business or banquets as the occasion arose. Recent excavations by Brian Hodkinson revealed evidence of a drawbridge and portcullis at the outer end of the entrance passage, which ran underneath the first-floor hall.

At the very bottom of Cooper's picture is an amusing glimpse of his three-cornered hat, as he gazes in wonderment at the strengths – and some of the weaknesses – of the tower. It had been partially, but not totally, dismantled in the Williamite wars of 1690–91. More humiliating still was its further destruction by a 'stern old Puritan', one Solomon Newsome by name, who used gunpowder in 1760 in an effort to destroy the castle, because the sparrows nesting in its ivy were ruining his barley, and disturbing his sleep with their chattering dawn chorus. Fortunately, like the Williamites, he too failed to demolish the tower, but one suspects that the hole that Cooper shows near the top to the left of the machicoulis may have been one of the results of his efforts.

AC. delin. 16.ª June 1784   Print.ª 11.ª July

A N; View of **Nenagh** Castle ~ Co.ᵗ Tipperary ~

OLD CHURCH AT KILLALOE, Co. CLARE

In his diary for 22 May 1781, Cooper becomes expansive, if not exactly chatty, about Killaloe and its two main churches: the cathedral, and what we now call St Flannan's Oratory seen in the drawing opposite. Killaloe, he explains:

> ... is a small town situated on the side of a steep hill sloping down to the w.side of the river Shannon; over which is a bridge of 19 Arches. The only remarkable thing here, or what makes it a place of any note; is the Cathedral.... A few yards N.W. of the Cathedl. stands a small oblong Old building called the Killaloe, all stone work & is used to keep various articles. From the Name given this I suppose it to be part of the original Cathedl. & perhaps one of the oldest pieces of Masonry in the kingdom.

Citing O'Halloran's *Introduction to the Study of the History and Antiquities of Ireland* (Dublin, 1772), Cooper continues:

> At Killaloe in the most ancient building there, adjoining to the Cathedral, & which I have proofs was a Mausoleum, we see, at the old entrance on the W. of it, now shut up, the arch supported by two pillars, which tho' low, are covered with capitals of the Ionic Order.

He adds that Muirchertach O'Brien 'Kg. of Ireland' who died in 1119, 'pursuant to his commands when living', was buried there, as was also Dónal Mór O'Brien, 'Kg. of Limerick who is well known for his bounty and liberality' to many churches.

The church that is the object of Cooper's attention is the Oratory in the cathedral grounds which is best known for its stone roof, a feature probably imitated from Cormac's Chapel in Cashel. The doorway, blocked up in Cooper's time, has long since been re-opened, even if its capitals (one of which is carved with foliage) could scarcely be described as Ionic. Primarily a church, only secondarily, if at all, a 'Mausoleum', in Cooper's phrase, it may have been built around the middle of the twelfth century.

Cooper drew this picture some three years after his diary entry, presumably on a later visit. From the fact that his diary entry for Killaloe quotes not only O'Halloran but Harris's *Bishops* as well, we can deduce that he must have gone around the country with a well-stocked travelling library. Harris's *Bishops* refers to Walter Harris's 1764 translation of the works of Sir James Ware (including *The Bishops of Ireland,* a copy of which, in the Library of Trinity College, Dublin, was annotated by Austin Cooper's own hand).

A C: delin.t 16.th June 1784 —

Pinx.t 18.th July —

A S:W: View of the Old Church of Killaloe — Co.y Clare —

ABBEY AND CHURCH AT ENNIS, Co. CLARE

In the presence of a somewhat ragged cowherd, the head and shoulders of Austin Cooper at the centre bottom of the picture peer over a wall towards the venerable Franciscan 'Abbey' in the centre of the town of Ennis, Co. Clare.

Though founded by Donchadh Cairbreac O'Brien, King of Thomond, around 1240, the main church was not finished until around 1300. At this time, Donchadh's successor, Turlough O'Brien, furnished the building with 'sweet bells, crucifixes, a good library, embroidery veils and cowls', and donated glass 'painted in blue' for the triple-lancet window, which, sadly, Cooper's drawing shows to be open to the winds.

The south transept, seen ivied on the left, was added in the fifteenth century, when a cloister and a tower were built and further buildings were constructed, which do not now remotely resemble what Cooper shows to the right of the gable with the triple window. At the same time, the church was beautified by fine carvings depicting the dedicatee, St Francis, with his stigmata at the foot of the tower, and also carvings of various saints, and of the Passion, Death and Resurrection of Christ. Though the friary was officially suppressed in 1543, the friars were able to stay on for a considerable time, the last one not dying until 1617. The friary was re-established, but the friars were subsequently forced to leave several more times.

It was probably some time during the eighteenth century that the Established Church of the time decided to hold services in the friary and, for that purpose, re-roofed the nave. It must also have been at this time that the pyramidal roof over the remaining height of the central tower was added, giving it that very curious look shown in Cooper's drawing, so different to the tower with added storeys we see today. This tower, decorated with the prickly pinnacles, might have been erected when the Board of First Fruits granted aid for a church at Ennis in 1818. Though the pinnacles remain, the roof was removed when the Church of Ireland built its new church in Bindon Street in 1871. The friary, returned to the guardianship of the Franciscans in 1969, now stands open to public view in all its ruined glory, cared for as an historical National Monument by Dúchas, the Heritage Service.

AC: delin.t 17.th June 1784.   Pinxt 20.th July

A S.E: View of the Abbey & Church of Ennis *Co.y Clare*

CLOGHLEAGH CASTLE, Co. CORK

Surely none of Cooper's pictures distils better the essence and atmosphere of his travels around the countryside under armed guard than this vignette of Cloghleagh Castle in North Cork. He shows himself in his chaise, pulled probably by more than one horse, as he is surrounded back, front and sides by soldiers armed with guns, or pikes or swords – all belonging to the 10th and 46th Foot. These guards would have been necessary if, say, Cooper were travelling to Dublin with money gathered from the (tax) collectors in Cork.

Today, fast traffic moving along the same road from Fermoy to Mitchelstown quickly brings the motorist into sight of Cloghleagh Castle on the right, just after passing the agricultural station at Moore Park, and just before descending towards Downing Bridge, which straddles the River Funchen.

Cloghleagh Castle was built in the fifteenth or sixteenth century by the Anglo-Norman Condon family, which later identified itself strongly with the Irish cause. The Condons lost their lands after the Desmond Rebellion of 1587, but regained the castle in 1642. They apparently did this by persuading a shoemaker to allow himself to be caught with bottles of poteen by the soldiers of the castle. Having got them drunk, the sober and enterprising cobbler then opened a trap-door to admit the Condon contingent.

Sold to William Stephen Moore of Clonmel, Co.Tipperary, for £5,500 – a considerable sum in 1684 – the lands remained in his family until 1908. This family gave their name to the Park, and it was one of the family, Viscount Kilworth, who helped to keep the castle in such good condition by renewing the floors, repairing the roof and glazing many of the windows in the later nineteenth century.

A. W. View of Cloghleagh Castle - co. Cork -

ST MARY'S CHURCH, CALLAN, Co. KILKENNY

St Mary's in Callan is an example of a fine Kilkenny parish church, which has changed little since Cooper sketched it on 28 June 1784. It goes back to the thirteenth century, though the tall tower on the left is probably the only part of the original structure to survive. Most of the church as Cooper sketched it, and as it survives today, is a product of the fifteenth century.

The foreground is taken up with the exterior wall of the south aisle, for St Mary's is a church with an aisle on each side of the nave, the arcade between them being indicated by curious arches seen through the windows. The doorway displays fine carving too small in scale for Cooper to have detailed from a distance, and consisting of angels, interleaved vines and a lion. In the corresponding north doorway, not visible here, is a contemporary carving of a lady with a horned head-dress of a kind found on the effigy at Fertagh in the same county (no.3).

Cooper shows the chancel of the church as being roofed – as, indeed, it still is, although one may ask for how long? The church was used for Protestant services until the 1970s, but it is now boarded up and empty, except for a few tombstones and a fine medieval baptismal font.

Beneath the windows of the south chapel, shown here on the extreme right, is the grave of the parents of Edmund Ignatius Rice, the founder of the Irish Christian Brothers.

Abidelin.t 28.th June 1784   Simt.t 25.th July

A S, View of the Church of **Callan** Co: Kilkenny

AUGUSTINIAN FRIARY, CALLAN, Co. KILKENNY

On the opposite side of the River Nore from St Mary's parish church in Callan (no.69) is the Augustinian friary, founded by the Butlers in the fifteenth century. A long church with a tall tower rising within the walls almost halfway along its length, it has two unusual reticulated windows (one of which is seen here in the south wall), and a west doorway with a window above. The church is most notable for its fine sedilia, a set of niches in the south wall near the altar, which seat those officiating at Mass and which, in this instance, are decorated with leafy crockets above.

But the most colourful thing about the friary – other than the flags of the pitch-and-putt golf course outside it, the presence of which ensures the grass around the church is well trimmed – is one of the Butler family members associated with its foundation. Eamonn Mac Risderd (or Edward son of Richard) Butler and his wife had petitioned Pope Pius II for permission to found a friary for the Augustinians, but the process was rudely halted for a time when Eamonn was defeated in the Battle of Piltown in 1462. Being a well-known man of letters, Eamonn won his freedom by handing over two manuscripts, the Butler

Psalter (now in the Bodleian Library, Oxford) and the Book of the O'Mulconry's (now in the British Library, London) – both of which were written specially for him.

This must be one of the few instances recorded in Irish history where works of literature were accepted as ransom for a man's life – surely a very civilised form of warfare! However Eamonn's defeat lost him the honour of being founder of the friary, which was subsequently claimed by his son James who may have built the friary in atonement for having married his cousin, Sive Kavanagh, without a dispensation from Rome. Subsequent dispensation, however, allowed the couple to marry solemnly some years later in the presence of two of their children – one of whom was later to become the eighth earl of Ormond.

In the tradition of its near-founder Eamonn, the friary was noted for its learned community, and its library, rich in manuscripts, was said to have held a duplicate of all the rare works in the Cistercian library at Jerpoint. It also became the leading house of the Observantine reform movement late in the fifteenth century.

A S:W: View of the Friary at Callan — Co.y Kilkenny

LEIGHLINBRIDGE CASTLE, Co. CARLOW

When the English traveller Thomas Dineley crossed the River Barrow at Leighlinbridge in 1681, he noted in his diary that there was a fair bridge there 'with the Ruines of an Ancient Castle and Abbey belonging to his Grace the Duke of Ormond'. This refers to the bridge and impressive tower house seen in Cooper's picture; both show comparatively little change in the intervening centuries, except that the nearest corner of the tower has now collapsed.

Many historical sources say that Sir Edward Bellingham built the tower in 1547. However, in his recent book *The Medieval Castles of Ireland*, David Sweetman has refuted the records and has suggested that some of the existing structure formed part of an earlier tower, which might have been constructed for the Carmelites around 1320, to help them protect the bridge. The Carmelites later received royal grants to maintain the bridge – claimed to be the oldest bridge in the country.

But the friary must have consisted of more than just the tower because, when it was dissolved in 1542, a church was seized, as well as a belfry, a dormitory, a hall and two chambers. It may have been this dissolution that gave Bellingham the opportunity to fortify the tower we see today, forming the centrepiece of this riverside village on the Barrow, now pleasantly quieter since the construction of a by-pass some years ago.

AC: delint 30th June 1784   Finist 27th July

An E: View of Leighlin-bridge. Co: Carlow

EAST VIEW OF KNOCKMOY ABBEY, Co. GALWAY

Opposite is the first of a series of eight drawings in the album that Cooper copied from the architect William Leeson (see Introduction, p.13). Apart from his professional prowess, another of Leeson's claims to fame is the authorship of an article on how to plant trees with a plough, which was published in the Dublin Society's *Transactions* (1803). All eight of Leeson's originals are of the same monument – the great Cistercian Abbey of Knockmoy, which stands out rather starkly in an open and treeless landscape beside the River Abbert in East Galway.

The abbey was founded around 1190 by Cathal Crovdearg O'Conor, King of Connacht, and he was buried there on his death in 1224. One of his other great foundations was the Augustinian Abbey in Ballintubber, Co. Mayo, which was restored to its former glory by being re-roofed in 1966.

Knockmoy has not had the same advantage, but a glance at the drawing reproduced opposite shows how similar the two foundations are in the eastern view of the chancel. Near the right-hand side of Cooper's drawing, we see the east gable of the church, which has three round-headed windows grouped together, with one string course at the level of the bottom of the arching and another above. Further up the gable, we encounter one broader and one narrower round-headed window. The articulation is not exactly the same as at Ballintubber, but the two are architecturally close enough to suggest that they were contemporary, if not, indeed, built to a common design scheme, thirty or more years after the actual foundation of Abbeyknockmoy.

For an architect, Leeson's drawing betrays a curious treatment of the rules of perspective in that he has the string-courses of the east end disappear downwards, while the lines of the garderobe on the left disappear upwards into the background. His detailing of the extreme right-hand end (north transept) is not easy to understand, and a comparison of the drawing with that in the *Journal of the Royal Society of Antiquaries of Ireland* for 1904, shows that he has massed the various parts of the building too closely together. But for all that, it is an attractive vista, which, fortunately, has changed little since Leeson drew it in 1784.

Wil.^m Leeson delin.^t 1794.   AC Orme.^d 10.^t Sep.^t 1794.

An E: View of Knockmoy Abbey ~ Co.^y Galway ~

SOUTH-WEST VIEW OF KNOCKMOY ABBEY, Co. GALWAY

William Leeson, the draughtsman of the lost original copied here by Cooper in 1784, probably came from Loughrea only eighteen miles away and, therefore, had plenty of time to spend at Knockmoy, moving around and taking various views both inside and out.

In the south-west view reproduced opposite, the left-hand side of the picture is taken up with the nave of the church, and the three arches of its arcade. This is reasonably correct, even though the size of the west door and window above, in relation to the overall gable, is somewhat exaggerated.

But it is in the right-hand half of the picture that Leeson – doubtless intentionally – shows us things from a different perspective. The gable that we see with the doorway at first-floor level is meant to be that of the south transept, which should be at an angle of about 45° to that shown by Leeson.

The two fragmentary walls to the right of that gable are more difficult to match with what Leeson showed on the east elevation on the previous page. However, the building on the extreme right can easily be accepted as a part of the south range of the claustral buildings.

Essentially, then, what we have here is the south side of the church and sections of the buildings surrounding the cloister. At the centre of the picture are the somewhat shadowy pointed gables of the abbey choir – now roofed over by the Office of Public Works to help protect what remains of the pictures illustrated on subsequent pages. Finally, one of the interesting points about this view is that there is as little to be seen of a cloister arcade as there is today. Barralet's drawing of the abbey from the same angle, engraved in Grose's *Antiquities*, helps us to understand the monument better than Leeson's does.

Wil.ⁿ Leeson delin.ᵗ 1784

N.C. Prin.ᵗ 12.ᵗ Sep.ᵗ 1794

A S.W. View of Knockmoy Abbey — Co.ᵗ Galway

Copied these Views &c of this Abbey from the Originals in the Possession of Col.ᵗ Vallancey

PLAN OF KNOCKMOY ABBEY, CO. GALWAY

The advantage of visiting Cistercian abbeys anywhere in Europe is that you know exactly where you are and what you can see, because the layout is fairly standard. Of course there are always slight variations, but the basic plan usually consists of a church with its various connected buildings laid out around a roughly square cloister placed to the south. This knowledge helps us to understand the plan of Knockmoy opposite, as it was surveyed by William Leeson in 1784.

Standing, as it were, on the left, is the church with its nave hyphenated by an arcade left and right, linking with the aisles through a series of arches. Leeson's plan makes clearer than the remains existing on site today how the nave protrudes westwards beyond both the side-aisles and the external west wall of the claustral buildings.

The two chapels on either side of the vaulted chancel is typical of the Cistercian church layout. On the north wall of the chancel, 'A' marks the location of the painting of the Three Kings (see below no.78), while 'B' indicates what Leeson calls the 'Monument' (see below no.75).

The short transepts off which the side chapels open are, as Roger Stalley pointed out in his splendid book on *The Cistercian Monasteries of Ireland* (1987), probably modelled on the abbey at Boyle, Co. Roscommon, as are other details at Knockmoy. Stalley's plan of Knockmoy deviates from Leeson's particularly in the details of the cloister building. The most curious difference is the absence of a sacristy in Leeson's plan, which includes an extended U-shaped structure at the northern end of the cloister garth. This finds no place either in the existing remains nor in the standardised Cistercian plan.

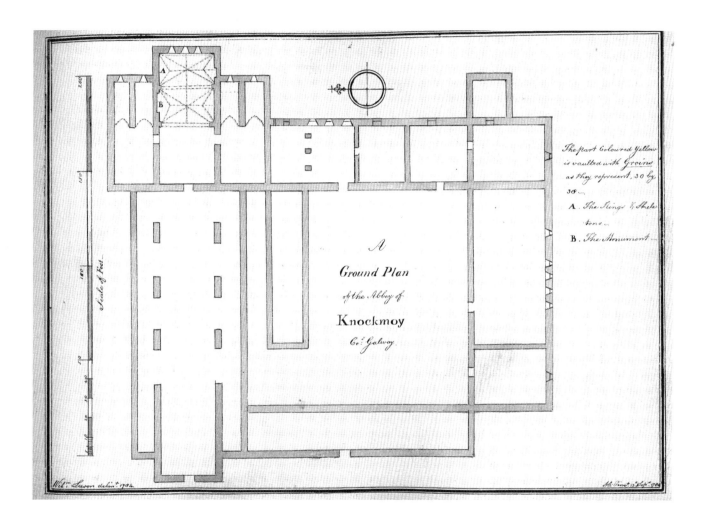

The Part Coloured Yellow
is vaulted with Groins
as they represent, 30 by
30.

A. The Kings & Skele-
tons.

B. The Monument.

Scale of Feet.

A

Ground Plan

of the Abbey of

Knockmoy

Co: Galway.

Wil: Lawson delin.t 1784.

Sc.t Print 15.t Sep.t 1784.

'MONUMENT', OR FRESCO PAINTING, AT KNOCKMOY ABBEY, CO. GALWAY

Marked 'B' on the plan of Knockmoy (no.74) is what Cooper calls the 'Monument' of the O'Conors, the family who founded the monastery. However the Monument is, more correctly, the early fifteenth-century O'Ceallaigh tomb (see also no.89).

Today, the tomb consists of a pointed arch, above which is a decorative cross. The cross has a small head beneath, while little turrets rise upright from the bottom of the arch. The arch itself is filled with masonry, and currently has three tombstones lying against it.

When William Leeson drew the ensemble in 1784 – the date given on the engraving of it in Ledwich's *Antiquities of Ireland* of 1790 – the arch was filled with a representation of the Crucifixion, which was probably added a century or more after the tomb was built. The iconography shows the Virgin with rayed head under the right hand of Christ on the Cross, and another figure turning away, who may well represent the Centurion.

On the bottom corners are two veiled figures who should probably be taken as the two Holy Women who came to comfort the Virgin. Underneath the bottom of the right-hand side of the arch and directly under the turret we see a panel with two figures who seem to be raising their forearms as they sit at a table. It looks as if the figure on the right is wearing a crown. It is possible that this is a misunderstood version of the two soldiers casting lots for Christ's garment, which are shown in roughly the same position in relation to the Crucifixion in, for instance, Giotto's Padua Crucifixion.

On the opposite side of the arch is a stone with an inscription, which is enlarged in no.89 below. Approaching the arch from the right is an apparently male figure with perhaps two female figures above – but none of the three would seem to be related to the Crucifixion. Beneath the upper right-hand figure there is an inscription, which is illustrated in no.76 overleaf.

N.º page 77

N.º 4
page 90

For the other Half
of this Monument
See page 79

Wil: Leison del.¹

Ho: brou. 25. Aug. 1785.

The Monument in Fresco Painting in the Abbey of Knocmoy (Co. Galway) of OConnor
the Founder

165

INSCRIPTIONS ON THE 'MONUMENT' AT KNOCKMOY ABBEY, Co. GALWAY

This and the following page provide us with the inscriptions that were once visible on the north wall of the chancel in the Abbey of Knockmoy, Co. Galway. The inscriptions reproduced opposite come from two separate locations. The first is from the Monument (the early fifteenth-century O'Ceallaigh tombstone).

Cooper writes over the first inscription: 'All that remains over the Monument'. He also marks the location of the original of this as 'no.1 on page 77' on the upper right of no.75 (that is, underneath the large right-hand figure above the arch). Because it is one of the rare Irish instances of a painted Gothic inscription in an alphabet known as Black Letter, it is sad that it is impossible to make out anything of this inscription – either what is shown on no.75 or on the half-size copy reproduced opposite. Obviously, even in 1784, the writing was almost illegible and, understandably, Mr Leeson, who drew the original, was not sufficiently conversant with the nature of Black Letter inscriptions to even to be able to make a sensible stab at the letters.

The lower of the two inscriptions opposite comes from a different monument on the same wall – the paintings of the Three Dead and Three Live Kings (see below no.78). The inscription comes from beneath the three skeleton kings (at the place marked 'no.2, page 77' on the illustration reproduced here as no.78).

In the 1850s, George Petrie, the founding father of Irish archaeology, had visited the site and had sent his son up a ladder to read the inscription, but the results were not very satisfactory. However, half a century later, Henry S Crawford examined the inscription again and, with the aid of the then-young RAS Macalister, was able to come up with a more satisfactory reading, which made sense when its location beneath three skeletons is taken into account. Their version reads:

Fuimus ut estis vos eritis ut sumus nos

which, roughly translated, means:

We were as you are, you will be as we are

Knowing now that this chilling message is a reminder of what faces all mortals, it is just possible to make out some of the letters in the version that Cooper gives us here.

Inscriptions on the Monument in the Abbey of Knockmoy, Co. Galway, see pages 76 & 79

INSCRIPTION ON THE 'MONUMENT' AT KNOCKMOY ABBEY, Co. GALWAY

Above the inscription reproduced opposite, Cooper has written: 'Under the Criminal, no.3 page 79'. This refers to the figure whose body is pierced with arrows by an archer on either side on the painted composition (discussed in more detail overleaf).

Like the two previous inscriptions (no.76), this one is written using the Black Letter alphabet, which was popular in tomb sculpture in Ireland, particularly in the fifteenth and sixteenth centuries. Again, it is virtually impossible to make them out on the basis of the drawings reproduced here. But, once more, Henry S Crawford comes to our rescue, having read the inscriptions carefully when they were more visible than they are now. His version reads:

Orate p‾aiab malachie o Nollain et Conhuir hi eddichan qui me fieri fecit

which, translated into modern terms, reads:

Pray for the souls of Malachy O Nolan and Conor O Heddigan who had me made

This indicates the names of the two men who wanted to commemorate the fact that they had commissioned the painting. Sadly, no one has yet satisfactorily identified the two men and, since they are not historically known personages, we are not in a position to date the mural with any certainty.

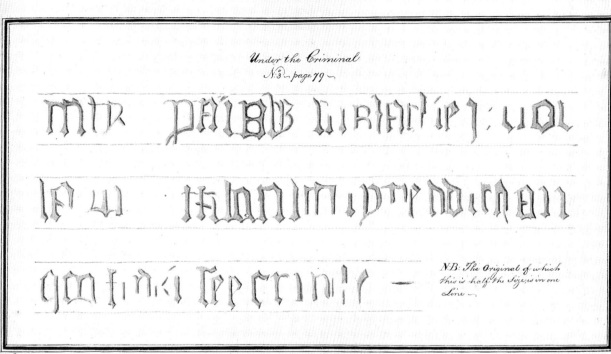

Under the Criminal
N.º 3 page 79

N.B: The Original of which
this is half the Size, is in one
Line

Wilᵐ Leeson delinᵗ 1784

Alex Bindᵗ 10 Sepᵗ 1784

Inscription on the Monument in the Abbey of Knockmoy. Coᵗ Galway. See pages 76 & 79

'MONUMENT' AT KNOCKMOY ABBEY, Co. GALWAY

In the neighbouring niche to the O'Ceallaigh tomb at Knockmoy (no.75), there is a series of painted figures, placed in two registers, one above the other, in the recess marked 'B' on the plan (no.74). The top row shows three crowned skeletons, and three live crowned kings – one with a falcon, the second with a plant and the third with a bird and a sword.

Edward Ledwich, who had the original of this Leeson drawing engraved for his *Antiquities of Ireland* (1790), saw the middle figure of the latter group as Roderic O'Connor (the last High King of Ireland and the brother of the founder of Knockmoy), holding some shamrock. In fact, the grouping together of 'the three dead kings and the three live kings' is part of a well-known genre, which may have derived from a French morality play, popular in the fourteenth century. That this play was common at the time is known from a number of frescoes of roughly the same period in England – and this could suggest a date perhaps in the late fourteenth or the first half of the fifteenth century for the Knockmoy picture. On the English examples, the three dead kings are often accompanied with a similar verse to that discussed in no.76: namely, 'we were as you are, as we are so you shall be'.

The second row of figures forms two separate groups, unrelated to the scene above. On the left is a seated figure, usually taken to be God the Father, possibly holding a scroll. To the right, two archers are firing arrows at a figure tied to a tree-trunk between them. Though not certain, the most likely interpretation of the figure pierced with arrows is St Sebastian, popular from the early fifteenth century onwards as a patron saint to whom one could pray in time of plague. Running most of the way across the bottom of these two unrelated paintings is the inscription mentioned above (no.77) asking a prayer for the souls of Malachy O'Nolan and Conor O'Heddigan, who had presumably commissioned the pictures.

These figures have sadly all but disappeared, yet traces of green, brown and perhaps yellow were still visible in 1917 and, in the late nineteenth century, Sir William Wilde saw that the archers wore tight yellow hose and greenish jackets. But when experts re-examined the painting in 1989, they added blues and greens to the usual red and yellow palette. In their view, this was not a fresco, but what they described as a 'line--painting' dating, they thought, from around 1500.

For reasons of preservation, the chancel of Knockmoy is normally kept locked, so that the paintings are not accessible to the casual visitor.

N.º 2 page 77

N.º 3 page 78

The Monument &c in Knockmoy Abbey Co.ᵗ Galway Continued from page 76

ROUND TOWERS AT KELLS, CO. MEATH (A), AND CLONES, CO. MONAGHAN (B)

These Round Towers demonstrate the fact that the genre continued to hold a fascination for Austin Cooper over a number of years, since he had, apparently, sketched the Kells tower in 1784 and the Clones tower three years later. However, there is some mystery surrounding these dates. The year 1797 is clearly shown on the bottom left of the right-hand circle (the Clones tower), but this is out of line with the following pages, which are dated 1785, and the preceding pages, which are dated up until June 1784. Did Cooper make a small mistake with the last two digits, or did he deliberately leave an open space on the appropriate page in 1785, which he then completed twelve years later? In support of this theory, it is obvious that there is a difference in style between the two towers, in that Cooper has left out all background in the Clones depiction, but, unusually, has included the background wall in the Kells picture.

Unexpectedly, in the Kells picture, the tower is shown from the street, rather than from inside the churchyard, with the effect that we do not see the doorway. Instead, we are shown a gatepost and some steps leading down to street-level where the bollards shown here still stand. There is, in fact, a High Cross just over the wall, beside the tower. It has an inscription alluding to St Columba or Colmcille, founder of the family of monasteries that set up a new house in Kells in the first decade of the ninth century, after the Vikings had made two disastrous raids on the mother-house at Iona in the Inner Hebrides. However, there is not a sign of this cross in Cooper's drawing.

The Clones tower remains much the same as it was in Cooper's day. Standing in a churchyard just a few hundred paces from the centre of the town, it was associated with a monastery founded by St Tigernach, who died in 548. Here, too, High Crosses were erected in the monastery; a shaft and a head, each from a different cross, are mounted one on top of the other in the centre of the Diamond. Near the foot of the Round Tower, there is a twelfth-century stone sarcophagus said to mark the grave of the founder, and there are also some eighteenth-century tombstones with horse-riders, cannon and hourglasses – products of a local school of masons and well worth admiring. However, once again, nothing of these is to be seen in Cooper's picture.

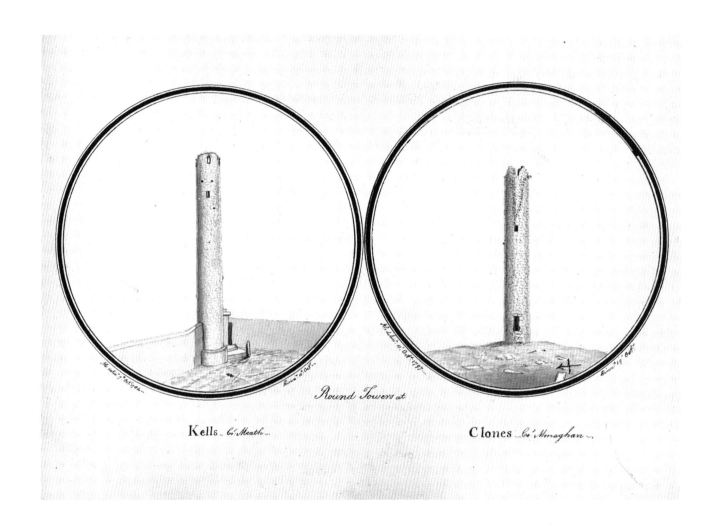

Round Towers at

Kells _Co. Meath._ Clones _Co. Monaghan._

DUNSHAUGHLIN CHURCH, Co. MEATH

The church that Cooper drew at Dunshaughlin, on the Dublin–Navan road, obviously consisted of two parts. The older section, ruined and perhaps dating from the thirteenth century, stands on the right, while a later portion, probably built in or not long before the eighteenth century, occupies much of the centre of the picture. Could we but read the inscription that presumably was written upon the plaque shown above the door, it would have been easier to offer a date. But in roughly the same position above the doorway today is a more recent tablet bearing the words:

This Church and steeple was rebuilt and Ornamented in the year of our Lord 1814. The Revd William Irvine Rectr

Mess. Gorges E Irvine and James Dempsey Church Wardens. By James Graham of Dunshaughlin Mason.

The present church is, therefore, obviously a rebuild of that shown by Cooper. It now has three windows instead of two, and the tower is now taller and thinner with an offset just above the level of the church. Instead of the three windows Cooper shows on the older part of the church, all we have left now is an arch and a half, against which leans a lintel bearing a Crucifixion scene, which is probably twelfth century in date and, therefore, older than any of the other remains. It is the one link with the early medieval church-site associated with St Seachnaill, which may have been founded in the time of St Patrick.

AC delin 5 Oct 1784

Pinot 10 Oct

The Church of Dunshaghlin, Co. Meath

ST MARY'S CHURCH, DROGHEDA, Co. MEATH

In 1778, when Cooper was nineteen and first sketched St Mary's Church in Drogheda, he may well have been painting smaller pictures, which might account for the reduced scale of this illustration when compared with others in this volume. His unusually long and informative caption is worth quoting:

> A view of St Mary's Church in Drogheda including that part of the Town Wall where Cromwell made a Breach & took the Town by Storm in 1649. Taken from the opposite Hill where he erected his Battery.

This helps to elucidate at least some features of the picture. If taken from the 'opposite hill' where Cromwell had his battery, the view must have been sketched from the east. The wall in the foreground must have overlooked the steep-sided valley that Cromwell's troops crossed to get through the town wall here, before beginning his slaughter of the citizens – an event that has never been forgotten in Irish folklore.

The central arch of the church must have belonged to a tower at the crossing, with north and south transepts seen on either side. The windows in the north transept (on the right) appear to be in the style of the thirteenth century. Presumably this was the church of the Carmelite priory founded here during the reign of King Edward I (1272–1307) although, at the Reformation, the jurors reported that, at that time, all the priory's buildings had been thrown down.

The tall tower in the left background may mark the site of the Duleek Gate shown on a seventeenth-century map. It is probably part of the town wall indicated by crenellated battlements in the background of Cooper's picture.

H. delin.t 25.th Dec.r 1770

Finn.t 8.th April 1785

A View of S.t Mary's Church in Drogheda including that part of the
Town Wall where Cromwell made a Breach & took the Town by Storm
in 1649 — Taken from the opposite Hill where he erected his Battery —

YELLOW STEEPLE, TRIM, CO. MEATH

The town of Trim is dominated by two ruined medieval structures, the castle (seen on the following page) and the Yellow Steeple, which faces it across the River Boyne. In fact, Cooper's drawings of these two buildings were taken from almost the same spot. The Yellow Steeple is the sole remnant of an old monastery that adopted the Augustinian rule of Arrouaisian observance around the middle of the twelfth century, though the structure itself was built no earlier than the fourteenth century. Although it has lost much of its western side, it retains an elegant appearance, which derives from its very gradual reduction in size above each of its string courses.

In his diary, Austin Cooper complains about a description and illustration of the tower in *The Gentleman's Magazine* of February 1784, and says that even the half that now remains is 'one of the handsomest buildings I have seen & much the highest of its kind in Ireland'.

During the medieval period, the abbey was best known for a miracle-working statue of the Virgin, widely referred to as 'the idol of Trim'. This statue no longer exists, having been consigned to the flames by reforming zealots in 1538. Somebody – probably a descendant of Austin Cooper's with the same name – wrote the following, inserted on the page opposite the drawing of the Yellow Steeple:

The Yellow Steeple (the tower of St Mary's Abbey) 125ft high was built about 1370, and is stated to be the most lofty monument of the Anglo-Norman architecture now existing in Ireland. There is a tradition that Cromwell battered down a portion of this tower, and there is scarcely a ruin along the Boyne from this to Drogheda which is not said to bear evidence of his cannon. A *cloictheach* or Round Tower formerly existed at Trim, the burning of which by Conor O'Melaghlin, in 1108, and by Conor Feargal O'Lochlinn in 1127, is mentioned in several Irish annals.

AC delin 15th May 1788   Sent 21st May

The Steeple of the Abbey of Augustines at Trim.
Commonly called The Yellow Steeple. Co^y *Meath*.

TRIM CASTLE, Co. MEATH

Trim Castle on the River Boyne looked like a pleasant, romantic, ivied ruin when Cooper sketched it in 1785 but, in its prime, it was one of the most impressive of all fortifications to bear witness to the Norman domination of Ireland in the twelfth and thirteenth centuries.

To make the castle's defences more impressive, waters from the Boyne (shown here on the bottom left) were partially diverted around the back to turn it into an island fortress. Thus the castle was reachable only by boat from the Boyne, or by land through one or other of the two smaller gate-towers, seen here on the skyline. But the main feature of the castle is, of course, the massive donjon at the centre, where the great Norman baron, Hugh de Lacy, and his successors would have lived and held court. Hugh's first fortification here had been swiftly burned by the native Irish, who had strongly resisted these new invaders, but, by 1175, de Lacy had started to build the central, tall tower we can still see today.

The science of dendrochronology, or tree-dating, which can tell us how old a piece of wood was when it was cut down, means we can be fairly precise about when Trim Castle was built. Pieces of wood from the original scaffolding that were found recently in the outside wall of the tower provide late twelfth-century dates. Further fragments of wood obtained from higher up show that building continued on till at least 1204, though it may well have been much later in the century before the tower reached its final form.

In plan, the tower was in the shape of a Greek cross. The fact that this style would have offered any potential attacker enough handy angles from which to undermine the structure suggests that style and the desire to impress were competing with defence considerations in the design and layout of the castle.

Kevin O'Brien's exciting reconstruction drawings, reproduced in David Sweetman's book *The Medieval Castles of Ireland* (1999), shows what the tower looked like in its heyday. The book also shows the workings of the drawbridge in the rounded gate-tower on the left of Cooper's picture. This, together with its counterpart in the centre right of the picture, gave access to the castle. The only other entrance would have been in the wall alongside the River Boyne.

Again it is Kevin O'Brien's reconstruction drawings, based on the results of Alan Hayden's excavations (1995 and 1996) that help to clarify what the buildings in the right foreground originally were. On the extreme right was a corner tower in the curtain wall that once enclosed the whole castle area, and the heavily ivied building to the left of it was a great two-storey hall with large windows on the upper floor, which looked out over the Boyne. The ivied tower almost in the centre of the foreground was the mint for making coins. The original curtain wall between it and the north-eastern corner tower at the extreme left of the picture had almost entirely disappeared even in Cooper's day.

A N. View of the Castle of Trim — Co. Meath

ABBEY OF NEWTOWN TRIM, Co. MEATH

The Abbey of Newtown Trim is no mean building when compared to Trim Castle and the Yellow Steeple, which dominate the skyline to the west, about a mile upstream along the Boyne.

The original church, allegedly built in four years, was more than 200ft in length, making it into one of the largest examples in medieval Ireland. This fact, however, is not easy to appreciate, as only a part of it survives, and even that part is somewhat confusing. To make matters worse, the angle shown here in Cooper's drawing is not that normally seen by the visitor, who would approach the church from the far end – through a graveyard with a second ruined, and very much smaller, parish church. This church contains a fine Elizabethan double effigy of the Dillon family, dating from 1586. What the left-hand half of Cooper's picture shows is the former choir of the church, with vast gaps in the north and south walls.

Originally, the 120ft-long nave of the church would have taken up most of the right-hand half of the picture. However, this was apparently demolished when the decision was taken to truncate the church to the size we see today, and create a new western end – which is the gable with door and two windows above that we can see just to the left of centre. What looks like pockmarks all over the gable walls (and even around the corner) are putlock holes for scaffolding, which

were never filled up after the masonry was completed. The lancet windows seen at the eastern end of the choir on the extreme left belong to the original church, which must have had, or was at least intended to have, a great stone vault that would have rivalled that of Christchurch Cathedral in Dublin.

The Abbey, which was dedicated to St Peter and St Paul, was founded by Simon de Rochfort, Bishop of Meath, in 1206 for those Augustinian canons who followed the rule of St Victor of Paris. De Rochfort probably chose that particular congregation because, while they owed obedience to their prior, they were not exempt from the jurisdiction of the bishop. De Rochfort also intended this grand building to become the new seat for his diocese of Meath, which he moved here from Clonard, so that, for a time at least, Newtown Trim functioned as a cathedral.

The building on the extreme right of Cooper's picture is the late medieval guesthouse, which is no longer as well preserved as is shown here. The buildings between it and the church comprise parts of the chapter house and also the frater, or refectory, which is built above a ground floor foundation. Its windows give a fine view over the River Boyne. If viewed from a gate across the river, those windows also provide a wonderful echo, which is worth trying out on the unsuspecting!

A N.W. View of the Abbey of Newtown near Trim. Co.y Meath

PRIORY OF ST JOHN THE BAPTIST, NEWTOWN TRIM, CO. MEATH

Newtown. The Priory of St John the Baptt. at Newto. stands on the S. side of the river a little below the Abbey before-mentioned, close to a bridge over the river. The ruins are extensive & not remarkable for regularity of stile; neither has it any great religious appearance – a square Case. [Castle] stands next the bridge & from it run a regular range of building along by the Water's edge to another Case. at the E. end, beside wch. stands the E. window of a small Chapel, of a light Triple form. There are some other pieces of walls in a large Orchard adjoining & on the road side near the Case. aforementd. stands a very neat built turret of an octagon form.

Thus runs the commentary in Austin Cooper's diary for 15 May 1785, dealing with the ruins of the Priory of St John the Baptist at Newtown Trim, which he sketched that day.

The four-arched bridge, which forms the forefront of the picture, may well be medieval in date, though it has probably been repaired to serve the modern road traffic that passes over it (suitably controlled by traffic lights, because it was designed to take only a single carriage).

Standing behind it is the Priory of St John the Baptist, once a community of the Crutched Friars. This Order gets its unusual name because its members bore a Crux, or a cross, either carried in their hands, or embroidered in red on their white habits, or both. Obscure in origin, the Crutched Friars were an Order of Hospitallers devoted to the care of the sick and the poor. Unlike the Knights Hospitallers of St John of Jerusalem, they were not military in character. They had more than a dozen houses scattered throughout Ireland. Together with another of their houses at Kells, this priory must have served as the main medieval medical centre in Co. Meath.

Perhaps the specific hospital function helps to explain why the layout of the buildings, which may seem somewhat higgledy-piggledy to the modern eye, does not conform to the usual monastic ground plan. The function of rooms as wards for patients would probably have taken priority when the layout was designed. Most visible are the two rectangular towers, that seen on the left of Cooper's drawing being at the eastern end of the riverside range of buildings. The other – nearer the bridge – may have been erected by the prior as his domestic quarters. But both of these buildings look more fifteenth than thirteenth century in date. Perhaps they were erected with the aid of an indulgence granted in 1402 for the repair of the hospital, at which time the church – by now rather ruinous – would probably also have benefited. The small turret on the right may have been a watchtower of some kind.

A.C. delin 15.ᵗ May   Pinxᵗ 24.ᵗ May

1785

The Priory of S.ᵗ John the Baptist at Newtown *near* Trim *Co.ʸ Meath*

NEWHAGGARD CASTLE, Co. MEATH

Newhaggard is situated on the south side of the River Boyne, only a few miles west of Trim on the Kinnegad road. A large nineteenth-century mill on the opposite bank shows how important the river was as a source of power. If the Boyne was navigable up as far as Trim, as we know it was, boats could also have plied those extra few miles upstream to Newhaggard – which would help to make the presence of this curious building a little more understandable.

Cooper's drawing makes it clear that there is a tall entrance on the north side (here he usefully indicates the direction by a small compass arrow). This entrance, the blocking of which has obscured its original function, is matched on the south side by a similar arch, thus making it clear that this was an entrance, or gate-house. The ornamental arcade above the gateway on the side shown here, together with the machicolation on the corner, adds to its impressiveness. The windows indicate that there may have been living space above. The decorative face looked towards the Boyne which, before drainage, may have flowed much closer to the monument than it does now.

But if this building were an entrance gate for those travelling via the Boyne, the question is, what was it giving access to? Alan O'Connell, who lives nearby in the Georgian-era Newhaggard House, says that there is a large dyke on higher ground to the south. This could suggest the presence of a medieval settlement of some sort, but as this structure has no curtain wall abutting onto it, it may have been created to act as a kind of ceremonial entrance to whatever lay behind it.

R. delin 15th May

1785

Engd 1st June

Castle of Newhaggard ~Co.y Meath~

DONORE CASTLE, Co. MEATH

Donore Castle lies close to the north bank of the River Boyne, strategically sited near a bridge on the Trim–Kinnegad road. A chapel and a friary belonging to the Dominicans are sited close to it on old maps. The likelihood, therefore, is that the castle was part of a small settlement that could have been under the protection of Trim, only half a dozen miles away.

Although it appears to be a tower house much the same as any other, except for the small corner turret shown in Cooper's illustration, Donore has assumed an importance beyond its status. This is because in Harold G Leask's *Irish Castles and Castellated Houses* (1941), it is used as *the* example of a so-called £10 Castle.

In the year 1430, King Henry VI offered a grant of £10 to anyone who would build a castle or tower sufficiently embattled and fortified, and to specific dimensions, in order to fortify the Pale, a rather movable border outlining the area of English domination surrounding the city of Dublin. The dimensions given were: a minimum 20ft in length, 16ft in breadth and 40ft in height. But there may not have been enough takers, as another grant offered in 1447 – confined to the Liberty of Meath – reduced the internal dimensions to 15ft x 12ft x 40ft. The measurements for Donore are marginally larger than those prescribed by the 1430 Act and, given that the narrow windows could well belong to the mid-fifteenth century and support the notion of a tower built for defence, Leask's suggestion that Donore is one of the '£10 castles' deserves serious consideration.

The fact that the castle was roofed – probably with thatch in Cooper's day – suggests that it was lived in 200 years ago, but its inhabitants can't have enjoyed well-lit interiors, and the door does not look as if it were capable of keeping out draughts. However, is that not a long stack of turf piled up in front of it for the winter fires?

Castle of Donore ~ Co.^y Meath ~

DEVENISH, Co. FERMANAGH

Devenish, a foundation of St Molaise in the sixth century, is the best preserved of Northern Ireland's monastic ruins, which makes it a popular goal for tourists today. But, situated on an island in Lower Lough Erne, only three miles below Enniskillen, it is also one of the most picturesque, which is why it was a popular subject for artists as far back as the eighteenth century.

The style of Cooper's drawing reproduced opposite is not his own, suggesting that he was copying the work of another draughtsman, though it is unusual for him not to name his source when he is copying a picture. The view has a remarkable similarity to one engraved by Sparrow in 1794 for Vol. II of Grose's *Antiquities of Ireland*, which states that it was 'taken from an original drawing in the collection of the Right Honourable William Conyngham' – without saying who the original artist was. This would help explain why Cooper was himself unable to name the creator of the original. I venture to suggest that the artist was Gabriel Beranger, who visited the island on 16 June 1779, on commission from William Conyngham, and many of whose drawings were in the portfolio of the right honourable gentleman. The inclusion of a pair of Fermanagh hay-makers relaxing in the foreground is also very much in the style of Beranger.

What the panorama shows is a view of the ancient monastery from the eastern bank of Lough Erne, not far from where the ferry crosses to the island today. Since the creation of the hydro-electric generating station above Ballyshannon at the lower end of Lough Erne, the level of the lake has probably risen. This explains why the tongue of land on the left and the row of trees on the island shore are no longer visible. The Round Tower – probably twelfth century in date – dominates the landscape. It is now accessible all the way to the top, which provides the visitor with a wonderful panorama of the charming Fermanagh countryside.

Further up the hill are the fifteenth-century ruins of the church and tower of the Augustinian priory of St Mary's, and further down to the left is what we can only assume is the Lower Church, otherwise known as An Teampall Mór (the large church).

A surprising omission is St Molaise's House, a tall, stone-roofed reliquary shrine located between the Lower Church and the Round Tower. Beranger mentions it in his manuscript description of the monuments on the island and it is included in a drawing by the Italian artist Bigari, who accompanied Beranger on his trip to the island. Perhaps St Molaise's was left out as it was too small to be visible behind the Lower Church.

Holland 20. July 1785

A View of **Devenish** *in Lough-Earne — C.º Fermanagh*

INSCRIPTION ON THE 'MONUMENT' AT KNOCKMOY ABBEY, Co. GALWAY

The O'Ceallaigh monument illustrated as no.75 shows an inscribed stone, marked no.4, supporting the bottom left-hand side of the tomb-niche. There the inscription is shown as making up five lines, but reference is made beside it to 'page 90' illustrated opposite – where the inscription is clearer and more detailed, and occupies only four lines.

Unlike the other inscriptions from Knockmoy discussed on the preceding pages, this one was carved in relief upon a stone. This stone was extracted and brought to the great Dublin Exhibition of 1853, which action may have led to the partial collapse of much of the tomb. The stone was never replaced in its original position, being brought subsequently to Ballyglunin House for preservation. Its present whereabouts are not known.

Because the inscription is carved on stone, it is more legible than the painted inscriptions discussed above (nos.76–77) and can be read as follows:

DO MAELSECHLAIND UA CELLAIE
DO RIG UA MAINE 7 DFINNGUA

LAIND INGEN UI CHONCHOBUIR DO RIGNE
MATHA O COIGLE IN LEABUIG SO

or, in translation:

For Maelseachlainn O'Ceallaigh
For the king of Uí Maine and for Finnguala
Daughter of O'Conchobair
Matthew O'Coigle made this resting place

As king of Uí Maine, O'Ceallaigh, anglicised O'Kelly, was ruler of much of the ancestral territory of East Galway, and the *Annals of the Four Masters* tell us that he was a truly hospitable and humane man who 'died after a victory of penance' in 1401. His wife (we would perhaps call her Finola or Fionnuala today) died after a virtuous life only two years later, the same source tells us. The *Annals of Ulster* add that she was 'a woman that was a generous protector of the learned bodies of Ireland'.

Half the Size of the Original

Wil.ᵐ Leeson, delin.ᵗ 1704.

Al: pinx.ᵗ 4.ᵗ Sep.ᵗ 1705.

Inscription on the Monument in the Abbey of Knockmoy, Co.ᵗ Galway. See page 76.

TYRREL'S CASTLE, CELBRIDGE, Co. KILDARE

Co. Kildare is second only to Co. Meath in the number of drawings devoted to it in the two albums by Austin Cooper dealt with in this book – but sadly it beats its neighbour to the north in the quantity of those monuments that have since disappeared.

The Celbridge drawing is a copy by Cooper of one executed by his cousin Samuel Walker in 1778, and captioned 'Tyrrel's Castle at the Wood Mills near Celbridge, Co. Kildare'. It is a curious structure, with what looks like a roughly square tower on the left. At a curious angle to this is a smaller rectangular tower with small windows, which may have allowed light into a staircase within. Unusually, there is a set of open steps leading to a doorway on the first floor of the larger castle; on the lintel of the doorway there seems to be some carving. Above the first floor, there were at least two further floors, with a string course beneath the parapet and holes to let the rain-water drain away.

The unexpected stairway suggests that this really was more a mill than a castle or tower house, and Taylor's map of Kildare of 1783, only five years later than Walker's visit, talks of 'Terril's Ca. And Mills'. In 1513 an Exchequer Inquisition already refers to 'Tyrrell-ys-Myll' as being owned by the Aylmers of Lyons. The family owned the premises until at least 1654, when the Civil Survey noted the presence of the castle, and 'one Corne Mill and one Cloth Mill'. We can assume that some of the milling activity took place in the low building appended on the right. But even at that time the castle was already described as ruined, and when Lord Walter FitzGerald came to write a note about it in the *Journal of the County Kildare Archaeological Society* in 1911, it had totally disappeared, to be replaced by Temple Mills.

S.Walker delin
3.d Sep.r 1778

A.C.d.in.t
21. Sept. 1785

Tyrrel's Castle *at the* Wood Mills *near* Celbridge *Co.d Kildare*

ARDFINNAN CASTLE, Co. TIPPERARY

Writing in *The Irish Penny Journal* of 1 May 1841, George Petrie, the father of Irish archaeology, had the following to say of Ardfinnan Castle:

> The traveller must have been a dull and unobserving one, who, journeying between Cork and Dublin by way of Cahir, has not had his attention roused by its romantic features, and an impression of its grandeur and picturesqueness made upon his memory, not easily to be effaced. Ardfinnan is indeed one of the very finest scenes of its kind to be found in Ireland, and is almost equally imposing from every point from which it can be viewed. The Castle crowns the summit of a lofty and precipitous rock, below and around which the Suir winds its way in graceful beauty while its banks are connected by a long and level bridge of fourteen Arches, which tradition states is of coeval erection with the fortress, and which, at all events, is of very great antiquity. On every side the most magnificent outlines of mountain scenery form the distant back-grounds; and every object which meets the eye is in perfect harmony with the general character of the scene.

The circular tower with the little chimney rising from near its left-hand end may date from around the reign of King John in the early thirteenth century. It has walls about 6ft thick and a small projecting rounded tower visible here, which provided the staircase between floors. Shrouded in trees today, the remainder of the castle may be somewhat later in date. Parts of it survive despite a battering by Cromwell's cannon from the opposite side of the river in 1649.

The large ruined building, whose two gables are shown behind the central part of the curtain wall, has been demolished to make way for a modern house, and changes and renovations have been carried out to the castle as late as the 1930s. Fortunately the splendid bridge commented upon by Petrie is still there and in daily use, though the foreground is now taken up with a modern church and national school. The old church on top of the hill behind the castle – only partially roofed 250 years ago – was largely replaced by the Church of Ireland in 1907. It has since been de-consecrated and acts as a Scouts' Den!

The artist who drew this view in 1746 is the same Anthony Chearnley who lived at Burntcourt and whose two views of the Everard 'castle' were reproduced earlier in this volume (nos.58–59).

Anthony Chearnley delin.º 1744

A. Cooper fecit 23 Octr 1785

A S:W: View of Ardfinan Co.º Tipperary

Built reign of King John 1184

CHARLES FORT, KINSALE, Co. CORK

harles Fort, guarding one of southern Ireland's best
natural harbours at Kinsale, is the most impressive
military fortification ever built in Ireland.

It is more than just coincidence, then, that the original of
this drawing is not by Cooper but by Col. Charles Vallancey
(1725–1812), who began a survey of the defences and weaknesses on the east and south coasts of Ireland in 1776. He
carried out a survey specifically of Charles Fort in 1777–78
(doubtless the date of the original of our drawing) and was
later to become Director of Engineers in Ireland. Exactly 100
years previously, another engineer, William Robinson,
Surveyor-General of Ireland, and architect of the Royal
Hospital, Kilmainham, had set about realising plans to build a
great fortification at Ringcurran which, in 1681, was to be
re-named Charles Fort in honour of King Charles II of England.

The original idea for a fort of this size came from the earl
of Orrery. He knew only too well how the occupation of the
site by the Spaniards before the Battle of Kinsale in 1601 had
given them an advantage, but he also realised how vulnerable
the south coast of Ireland was after the Dutch had blockaded

the Thames estuary in 1667. He chose the location because it
could control the entry of ships into Kinsale, and disregarded
the fact that it could be fired on from higher ground to the
north. That was to be the fort's Achilles heel, for this
weakness was exploited by the Williamites in 1690, when
they pounded the supporters of King James II within, and took
the fort after a siege of only thirteen days.

Vallancey has managed to give a remarkably accurate
view of the fort, taken from the shore to the south-east. The
defences have remained much the same, though the barrack
buildings have been unroofed. The outsize English flag – and
the English domination it signified – were removed when the
castle was handed over to the Irish State in 1921. However, it
was to be more than half a century before Dúchas, the
National Monument Service, could conserve and present it in
its present splendid state to the public. Of course, since
Vallancey made this sketch around 1778, and Cooper copied it
about sixteen years later, the town of Kinsale, represented by
a few houses on the hills at the extreme left, has expanded
many times over.

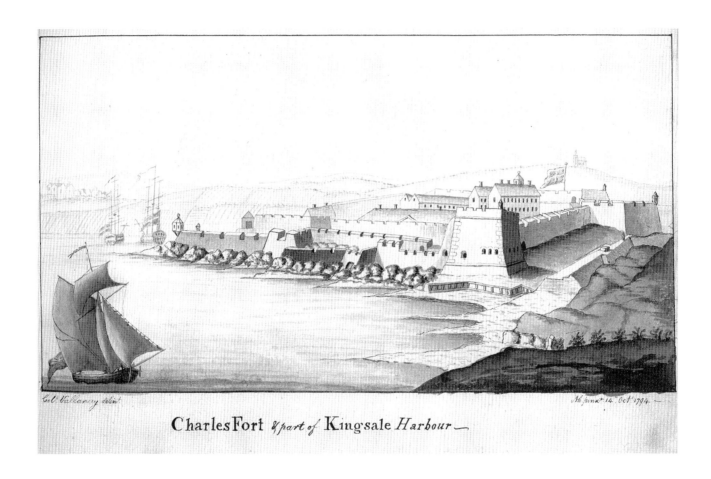

Col. Vallancey delin.   MB pinx. 14. Oct. 1794

Charles Fort & part of Kingsale Harbour

SOUTH-EAST VIEW OF MONASTERBOICE, Co. LOUTH

Monasterboice, several miles north of Drogheda off the road to Dundalk, is an old Irish monastery. Two of its High Crosses are among the most interesting and best preserved in the country.

St Buite, who died in 521, founded the monastery – allegedly on the same day that St Colmcille, or Columba, was born. This tradition may be invoked to recall links between Monasterboice and the Columban foundation at Kells, in the neighbouring county of Meath. The links are further hinted at by certain similarities in the High Crosses at both sites.

In her 1981 monograph on the site, the antiquarian Helen Roe has resurrected the account of how one Dominus Patrick McEgyr, the curate of a place named Salthouse, had 'sacrilegiously stolen the head of St Boice from the parochial Church of Monasterboith' in 1521. He was then arrested in Drogheda by Bishop Inge, who brought him to the arch-bishop's court at Termonfeckin. This was a fierce dispute over possession of a much-venerated relic but, though feelings ran

high, they fell just short of physical assault and the matter was settled out of court – after which, sadly, we hear no more of the whereabouts of the relic. The parish church from which it was taken was, presumably, one of the churches shown in Cooper's drawing – either the smaller one behind the left-hand cross or, more likely, that behind the right-hand cross. Traces of an arch can still be seen in the gabled wall of the right-hand building, making clear that this was a nave and chancel church. The fragmentary building on the extreme right is likely to have been the original chancel – could it even have been part of the shrine to house the relic of the founder?

Then, as now, headstones cluster around the church, but there is a large, apparently unused area between them and what is probably the cemetery wall in the foreground. An aerial photograph taken by Leo Swan revealed the boundary of the old monastery to have been much more extensive than today's wall. Incidentally, the house on the extreme left has completely disappeared.

A SE: View of Monasterboice Co: Louth

NORTH-EAST VIEW OF MONASTERBOICE, Co. LOUTH

Cooper's albums show he had a great interest in Round Towers, but an additional enticement to visit Monasterboice must have been the fine High Crosses, to which he devoted a second drawing. The Monasterboice tower itself was always considered important – an entry in the *Annals of Ulster* for 1097 states that the tower was burned with its books and many treasures, suggesting that one of the purposes of such Round Towers was to serve as the monastery's Treasury. But, surprisingly, eighteenth-century antiquarians usually paid little attention to High Crosses.

However, in the drawing reproduced opposite, Cooper is at pains to bring out the crosses in particular, making three ringed cross-heads stand out starkly against the skyline. Of the cross on the left, we see only a part of the head, though Cooper showed it in its entirety in a side view on the previous page (no.93). This is the famous Muiredach's Cross, which gets its name from an inscription carved on the base of the shaft. The inscription requests a prayer for a man of that name who had the cross erected, unfortunately without telling us anything further about him.

On its faces and sides, Muiredach's Cross has many naturalistic figures carved in high relief, illustrating scenes from the Old and New Testaments, culminating in what is one of the most splendid representations of the Last Judgement to survive from the first millennium. Stylistically, the cross may be ascribed to around the second half of the ninth century.

A similar date may be ascribed to the cross at the right of centre, near the Round Tower, known as the West Cross. The west face of this cross is one of the best preserved of all High Cross carvings, even if the religious subjects represented on it do present identification problems. The West Cross is also known as the Tall Cross because, at a height of more than 20ft, it is the tallest High Cross in Ireland.

There is also a third cross, shown falling to the left just over the wall in the centre of the picture. This may be the same cross-head that stands at roughly the same spot today. However, because the arms of the cross in Cooper's drawing project much further out beyond the ring than those on today's cross, the drawing raises the intriguing prospect that there may yet be another major cross-head still to be discovered at Monasterboice. The stump shown between the centre and right-hand crosses in Cooper's drawing may be the same currently preserved beside the centre cross in a railed enclosure in the north-eastern corner of the present cemetery.

A.C. delin.t 17. April 1786.   Eing.t 25. April 1786.

A N.E. View of Monasterboice *Co. Louth*

ABBEY AND CHURCH OF FERNS, Co. WEXFORD

Ferns, in north Wexford, was the power centre of Dermot McMurrough, King of Leinster from around the 1130s until his death at Ferns in 1171. Dermot's damaged reputation as the man who brought the Normans into Ireland has never been adequately countered by the good press he deserves for having founded, or assisted, a number of churches in his kingdom.

Preserved in the cathedral, which is at the centre of Cooper's picture, is a small fragment of a scalloped capital, suggesting that Dermot may have built a church on the site dating from around the middle third of the twelfth century. Very probably, he is also responsible for the ivied building with Round Tower on the left. This was part of an Augustinian monastery that was founded between 1158 and 1162, possibly to replace an earlier church burned in 1154, though the architectural historian Leask thinks that it looks older than the period of the fire. Other than the unusual fact that the Round Tower has a square base, the adjoining church is also interesting because its nave has a barrel vault with three transverse ribs. These are not visible behind the gable, which – like the other buildings in the picture – has now been cleared of its ivy.

Cooper's attention at the bottom of the picture is drawn more towards the cathedral at the centre, and the curious structure to its right. Cooper's drawing is historically valuable, and has been used by Sir Alfred Clapham to elucidate the very complicated building history of the cathedral, which was considerably altered in 1817. The square tower at the western end has been replaced by a taller, thinner one, and the east gable – between the original buttresses – is part of the modern refurbishment. What remains is the south wall of the choir, with the twin windows shown by Cooper.

One of the mysteries of this building complex is the purpose of the ivied building on the right. Its east gable, on the extreme right, has since fallen, but the north wall with its lancet windows indicates quite a large thirteenth-century structure. This would make it roughly contemporary with the Gothic cathedral, presumed to have been built here by the first Anglo-Norman bishop, John St John, who occupied the See from 1223–43, and who may be the subject of the episcopal effigy inside the current cathedral. At first glance, it might appear obvious that this structure was the original chancel of the cathedral, but the problem is that its floor has always been about 4ft below that of the cathedral, which has vaults beneath the present choir. Clapham suggests that this separated structure may have been the parish church for the town – at a lower level, naturally, than the bishop's cathedral!

A.C. delin.t 11.th June 1786 —   Paint.d 26 Aug.t 1787 —

The Abbey & Church of Ferns — Co.y Wexford —

TAGHMON CASTLE, Co. WEXFORD

The village of Taghmon would be a lovely, quiet place were it not for the traffic rumbling through it on the road from Foulksmills to Wexford town, which lies about eight miles to the east. It wasn't always a village for, in the medieval period, it was described in Holinshed's *Chronicles* as one of the towns of Co. Wexford – a Corporate Borough indeed, governed by a portreeve. The only survivor of its former military importance now, however, is the tower house, which rises to a height of four storeys above the town.

It is uncertain who exactly built the tower house. Perhaps it is natural that Wexford's great historian, Philip Herbert Hore (1841–1931) claims – with some justification – that it was a James Hore who erected it in the fifteenth century, paying his masons a daily rate of three halfpence or a peck of wheat.

In 1441 during the reign of Henry VI, an Act was passed 'for building towers upon the waters or River Taghmon in the County of Weysford'. It is difficult to be sure if this castle is a product of the Act because Taghmon is not on a river, nor does it have a harbour. But there must at least have been quite a bit of money available for its construction, as the Act enjoined that certain profits for services, forfeitures, marriages and rents were to be used for the building of the said towers and obstructing the waters. Certainly, in 1548, one William Hore was granted custodianship of the castle, but it is not clear if a single family inhabited it, as was usually the case with tower houses, or whether it served a small garrison for the Corporate Borough. It may never really have got over an attack on the town by disaffected Kavanaghs and O'Byrnes, who descended upon the town from Wicklow in the year 1600.

Taghmon Castle, Co. Wexford

SOUTH-WEST VIEW OF ROSCREA ABBEY, CO. TIPPERARY

As we know from Dennis Marnane's article in the *Tipperary Historical Journal* of 1993, Austin Cooper's brother Samuel – also a diarist – was agent to Lord Milton and his Damer family estate in Roscrea. This may help to explain Austin's extensive coverage of the antiquities of this important medieval town in the North Riding of his own native county of Tipperary. In addition to the Round Tower, St Cronan's Church and the castle (nos.62–64), as well as his copies of Barralet's view of the Round Tower (no.57) and his cousin Samuel's sketch of the High Cross fragments (no.111), Austin also made a drawing of what he called 'Roscrea Abbey' seen from the south-west.

Roscrea Abbey was, in fact, a Franciscan friary originally founded sometime in the third quarter of the fifteenth century. Its outstanding feature is the belfry which, along with the castle and the Round Tower, forms a trio of towers that pierce the skyline high above the town. It straddled the long hall church of the friars, and has only been able to survive virtually unaltered since Cooper's day because of the spirited action of an elderly lady who organised a chain of water buckets to put out a fire which broke out in the tower some time in the nineteenth century.

In the south wall of the church, Cooper shows an ominous-looking triangular gap, which must have subsequently expanded to such an extent that it brought down most of the wall, taking along with it the adjoining west gable, which Cooper's sketch shows as having a rather jagged-looking doorway with a window above.

In this book *Roscrea and District* (1976), George Cunningham quotes a medieval manuscript which states that in 1470, the Friars Minor gathered together in Roscrea in company with Eugene O'Carroll and 'invaded the fine church and new residence of their patron, Saint Francis' and carried away from it and elsewhere fine clothing and vestments – as well as beer and wine, though these, of course, may not have been the only reason as to why the friars went on the rampage and ransacked their own friary. But the inscription on a tombstone of 1523 commemorating another O'Carroll suggests that he may have rebuilt the friary, perhaps in atonement for what Eugene had done. But, if so, its useful life-span would have been even shorter, as the friary must have suffered the same fate as most Irish medieval monasteries in being suppressed by Henry VIII at the Reformation in the late 1530s, leading inexorably to its decline into the roofless ruin that Cooper saw, and that we can still see today.

AC. delin.t 17. April 1790   Pinx.t 5. Sep.r 1790

A S.W. View of Roscrea Abbey Co.y Tipperary

CARMELITE FRIARY, KILDARE

Kildare has been a town for many, many centuries and its ecclesiastical importance in the early medieval period rivalled that of Armagh and of Clonmacnoise. Its power was probably considerably strengthened and augmented in the early Norman period when William Marshall, Strongbow's son-in-law, built a castle there which, having been in the possession of the de Vesci family for a while, later became a FitzGerald stronghold. It is not surprising, then, to find that a number of friaries grew up to serve the citizens of Kildare in the later medieval period, among which were Franciscan (one of which was known as the 'Grey Abbey', illustrated earlier no.61) and Carmelite friaries.

The Carmelites were one of the four great Orders of mendicant friars who established themselves in Ireland during the thirteenth century. Though little is known of their early history in this country, we are quite well informed about their house in Kildare, which was founded in 1290 by William de Vesci. To judge by Cooper's drawing of 1790, reproduced opposite, it was a long hall church, with a row of lancet windows and stout corner buttresses. These would suggest that it may have been built around 1300, though its two broader east windows with simple, switch-line tracery may have been later alterations.

One of the friars, David O'Buge, himself a native of Kildare, where he is also buried, was described by Stanihurst in his description of Ireland (1584) as a man who was 'in philosophy an Aristotle, in eloquence a Tully and in Divinity an Augustinian'. When the friary was dissolved around 1540, it also had a belfry, a dormitory and a hall, but all of these had already disappeared when Cooper did his drawing in 1790. Not a trace remains of the church today, though the stone carved with the Crucifixion and an *Ecce Homo*, now preserved in Kildare's cathedral, may have come from the friary.

AC. delin.t 10.t Oct. 1790

A S:E: View of the Carmelite Friery at Kildare

MOTTE OF GRENOGE, Co. WESTMEATH

I had some difficulty in identifying the location of the Moat of Grenoge until the Midlands historian, Dr Harman Murtagh, pointed out to me that it was identical with that at Moate, less than ten miles east of his home town of Athlone. Sure enough, the most useful *Parliamentary Gazetteer* of 1846 calls the town Moate, or Moate-Grenogue, and Killanin and Duignan's *Shell Guide to Ireland* adds that it reportedly gets its name from 'Gráinne Óg, wife of one of the O'Melaghlins, the ancient ruling stock of Meath'. The *Gazetteer* waxes lyrically about the town, stating that:

> Travellers of all creeds and tastes can hardly fail to be refreshed with the balmy air which the town possesses, and the neat, tidy comfortable dress which it wears,' doubtless because 'a considerable number of families either are Quakers, or have taken from that people the tone of their character and manners.

Little of all that was in any way relevant to another, earlier group of visitors – Irish soldiers who, having abandoned the defence of Streamstown Pass at the height of the Williamite Wars in February 1691, fell back upon 'the Moote of Greenoge', followed by General Ginckel's Horse and Dragoons. There, according to George Story's *Impartial History of the Wars in Ireland* (London, 1693):

> A greater body of their Army was Posted upon the side of a Hill; and those also upon seeing what happened, retired into the Town; at the entrance of which, there was a very Defensible Ditch, with a Pallisado'd Work, which the Irish quitted, and March'd towards Athlone.

This hill is doubtless the Motte, seen from the west in Cooper's 1791 drawing, which is reachable down a lane leading southwards from the main street of the town. It is a mighty earthwork, erected by the Normans – possibly the Tuites – around the last quarter of the twelfth century and consisting of a well-defended motte in the shape of a flat-topped cone on the left-hand side and the raised bailey further to the right.

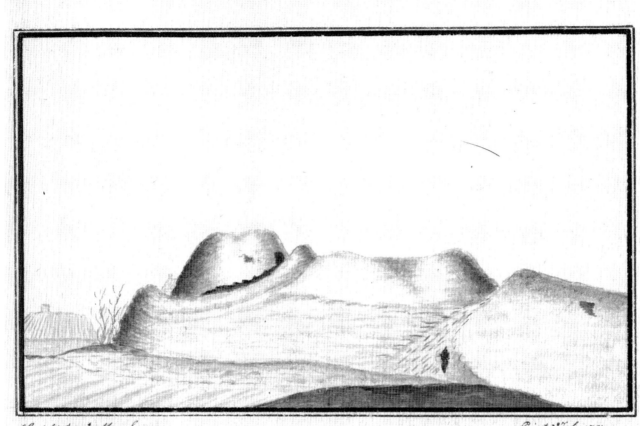

A.C. delin.t 29.t March 1791 —   *Print.d 3.d July 1791 —*

A W. View of the Moat of Grenoge — Co.y Westmeath —

EAST VIEW OF CREEVELEA, OR DROMAHAIR, Co. LEITRIM

The well-preserved Franciscan friary of Creevelea overlooks the River Bonet and can be reached on foot from the nearby village of Dromahair in Co. Leitrim. The *Annals of the Four Masters* record that one Owen O'Rorke and his wife, Margaret, founded the friary in the year 1508. This date makes it one of the last of the Irish Franciscan friaries founded before the Reformation struck. However, something else struck it even before the Reformation got to it – an accidental fire one night in 1536, which burned to death one of the friars and destroyed a great quantity of property.

The friars had been brought from Donegal, home of the Four Masters, and were joyful in recording their foundation at Creevelea. But the friars had to abandon the building at the Reformation, though they remained in the neighbourhood. They were allowed back at an exorbitant rent in the early seventeenth century, when they were permitted to re-roof part of the church with thatch. Twice more they had to leave and were able to come back again.

What Cooper shows is the view he would have had on approaching the friary from the village and, if you climb over the wall, the vista has changed little since Cooper's day. The focal point is the fine east window, with the upper part of the tracery looking like candle flames. The building to the left in Cooper's drawing is the south transept, while to the right of the traceried window are the sacristy and chapter room, and what may have been a 'sanitary annexe' to quote Leask's words.

What Cooper does not show is the existence of a cloister behind these walls. Its most interesting feature is the set of small carvings showing St Francis of Assisi demonstrating his stigmata, and talking to the birds, although you have to look closely to see them.

214

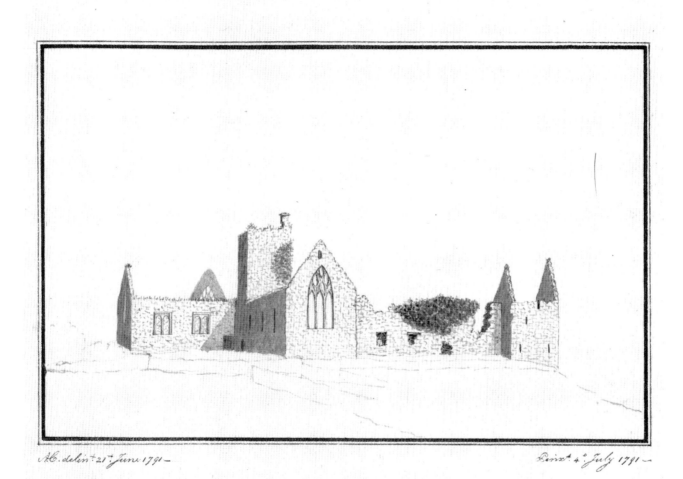

AC. delin.t 21.t June 1791 —   Pinxt. 4.o July 1791 —

An E. View of the Abbey of **Creevelea** or **Dromahare** — Co.y Leitrim —

SLETTY CHURCH, Co. LAOIS

Sletty is a peaceful site near the west bank of the River Barrow less than two miles upstream from Carlow town. The church in its present form looks to be late medieval in date. The position of the doorway, as shown by Cooper, is more central in the south wall than it is today, posing the question as to whether it has been restored, but using limestone instead of the original granite for the portal stones.

Probably centuries older than the church itself, however, are the two High Crosses that Cooper is careful to delineate to the left and right of the church respectively. The cross on the left has no ring and a pair of very short arms on a tall and narrow stem. Like the other one, it is undatable – but is almost certainly pre-Norman. The second cross, as Cooper intimates, is stockier, broader and has an unperforated ring. A circle at the centre of the head, too distant for Cooper to have recognised, may contain some decoration in the form of a cross of arcs or something similar – a motif that may well have been connected with relics or pilgrimage, or both, in early Christian Ireland.

These two crosses demonstrate the early medieval use of the site but they cannot indicate what made Sletty famous in the early years of Christianity, namely its connection with St Patrick. The founder of the monastery was a bishop, St Fiacc, said to have been converted from paganism by St Patrick himself. His name has been attached to a poem known as

Génair Patraicc, which, in the words of James F Kenney, is 'a metrical biography of St Patrick and one of the earliest hymns in the Irish language'. However, although the poem is likely to have emanated from Sletty, it was probably not composed until a few centuries after Fiacc's death.

Another name well known in the world of Patrician scholarship is that of Aedh, bishop of Sletty, who died in 700. He went to Armagh sometime between 661 and 688 and offered his kin and his church to Patrick forever, and may, thereby, have been one of the first to organise a *paruchia,* or a group of churches, associated with St Patrick. Through his influence on Muirchú, author of the seventh-century biography of St Patrick (which was dedicated to Aedh), Aedh can be given credit for propagating the cult of St Patrick – possibly with the hope of winning over the north of Ireland to the Roman way of calculating the date of Easter. Both Aedh and Muirchú attended the Synod of Birr together in 697, when Adamnan promulgated his law to exempt women from military service, and to protect children and clerics.

Sletty gives little indication nowadays that it was, again in Kenney's words, 'one of the chief churches of Leinster' in the early medieval period. Cooper was probably blissfully unaware of this fact when he sketched the later medieval church from below, in the terrain bordering the River Barrow.

AC delin. 8ᵗ April 1791

Church of **Sletty** *Queen's Coᵗ*

217

BOYLE ABBEY, Co. ROSCOMMON

The drawing of Boyle, Co. Roscommon, executed by Cooper in 1792, is unexpected, as it shows one of the less interesting panoramas of the great twelfth- or thirteenth-century Cistercian abbey. The view is taken from the Dublin–Sligo road as it passes through Boyle. When one looks at the winter date – 7 February – one realises that it may have been easier for Cooper to have sketched it from the comparative comfort of his carriage, than to get out and draw the building from a more interesting angle!

The blank masonry in the centre foreground is the west wall of the cloister area. But, as the doorway on the right neatly indicates, this does not belong to the original medieval abbey, but probably to a seventeenth- or eighteenth-century occupation of the cloisters as a barracks. That part of the building with the thatched roof is now unthatched, while the part with no roof between the gables further to the left has been restored by the Office of Public Works and the pointed doorway in it now provides access to the interior.

Belonging to the medieval abbey proper is the tower dominating the centre of the picture; it was inserted at the crossing of nave, choir and transepts after the construction of the church. The ivied part on the extreme left is the west doorway and gable of the church, finished about 1220. The monastery had been founded some sixty years earlier, and it took a lot of time and changes in the building style before the church was finished, with the completion of the west end shown here.

Described by Roger Stalley in his great book *The Cistercian Monasteries of Ireland* (1987) as 'the most attractive and rewarding Cistercian monument in Ireland', Boyle is a combination of west of England Romanesque and Transitional architecture. Its sculptured capitals are from a school of masons who worked on various buildings in the west of Ireland in the first third of the thirteenth century.

Abbey of Boyle Co.ª Roscommon

Taken from a hill which overlooks it

ROUND TOWERS AT DRUMCLIFF, CO. SLIGO (A), AND IN ANTRIM (B)

Once again, we have here a demonstration of Cooper's fascination with Round Towers, with fine examples from Drumcliff in Co. Sligo, and Antrim town. What is perhaps most remarkable about the drawings is that they were done only four days apart, which implies quite a speedy journey across Ulster in Cooper's horse-drawn carriage. (It also shows Cooper's penchant for drawing monuments not too far from the road!) Today tour buses congregate on the side of the Sligo–Bundoran road to pay homage to the tomb of WB Yeats – but all too often ignore the Round Tower at Drumcliff and the High Cross next to the path leading to the poet's grave.

Unusually – and fortuitously, since his diary entry for February 1792 has been lost – Cooper attaches the measurements of the tower to his drawing. He records, 'Door 1 foot 8 inches broad, 5 feet 2 inches high and 6 feet from the ground, plain and no architrave – Inside diameter of tower 9 feet 4 inches – Wall 3 feet thick'. He also illustrates a house abutting on to the tower, which is no longer extant. What he does not record is a local tradition that the tower will ultimately fall on the wisest man who passes it – and, though the upper half seems to have fallen already (on someone only half as wise?),

it is not yet too late to have your wisdom formally recognised and appreciated.

The other Round Tower in Antrim is a much more complete specimen, rising to a height of 92ft, though the conical cap was reset after the tower had been struck by lightning around 1820. The earliest known sketch of this tower, by the Welshman Edward Lhuyd, who visited Ireland in 1699, certainly showed the cap intact at that time. What is unusual about this tower is the ringed cross carved above the door, which Cooper noted as being about 6ft (in fact, it is 7ft) above the ground. It is rare to have any decoration on a Round Tower.

The tower stands rather isolated in a public park in Antrim town, and is the last survivor of an ancient monastery, which was probably already flourishing in the seventh century, and which seems to have had close connections with St Comgall's more famous foundation at Bangor on the southern shore of Belfast Lough. The date of either of the towers illustrated here is difficult to ascertain, but they are unlikely to be too far removed from the eleventh century.

Door 1 ft. 8 in.ᵈ broad, 5 ft. 2 in.ˢ high & 6 feet from
the ground, plain & no architrave —
Inside diameter of tower 9 ft. 4 in.ˢ —
Wall 3 ft. thick —

A.C. delin 9ᵗʰ Feb.ʸ 1792 —

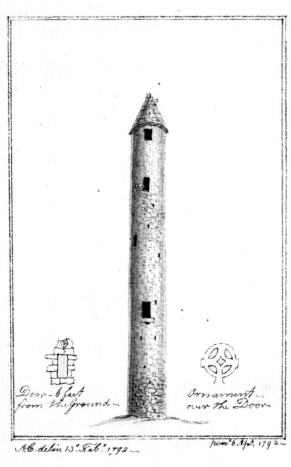

Door 6 feet
from the Ground —

Ornament
over the Door

A.C. delin 13ᵗʰ Feb.ʸ 1792 —   finisʰᵈ 6 Apᵗ 1792 —

Round Towers

Drumcliff ~ Co.ʸ Sligo

Antrim ~ Co.ʸ Antrim

BALLYMORE CASTLE, Co. WESTMEATH

I do not find anything Remarkable of this place in former times; it's only a small village upon the Great Road between Mullingar and Athlone, being ten miles distant from each. The place has always been very poor, and had only two or three Houses of Entertainment in it, the rest being all Irish Cabbins to the number of a hundred or thereabouts (though now there is neither House nor Cabbin standing.)

This is the description of Ballymore, Co. Westmeath, by the Reverend George Story, regimental chaplain, in his *An Impartial History of the Wars of Ireland* (published in London in 1693), which gave details of the Williamite campaign in Ireland in 1690–1691.

The houses shown in the background of the sketch by Samuel Walker (which Cooper copied in 1792) show that considerable improvement had been made in the hundred years since Story's account. A further two centuries on, Mr Story would scarcely recognise the village: The houses are now generously spread over its mile-long east-to-west main street, and they are neat and well kept, as are the fields and hedges surrounding them.

Standing about a hundred yards to the south of the village street is a stout, round castle which, from a distance, could easily be mistaken for a windmill. It is only when you peep inside that you realise that this is not for a Don Quixote, but a real-life fortification with walls up to 8ft thick. The door – now not so well preserved as in Cooper's day – leads into a round room with stone-domed ceiling, and stairs ascending in a slow spiral within the thickness of the wall.

The castle is said to have been built by a Norman family, the de Lacys, in 1309. The date may be roughly right but, though the de Lacys had earlier owned the land on which it stands, it is more likely that the castle was built by the D'Altons. However, it subsequently changed hands many times before it was abandoned after its one and only appearance in the pages of history – of which more overleaf in relation to illustration no.105.

J. Walker delin.   AC. pinxt 9. April 1792

Castle of **Ballymore** Co. *Westmeath*

BALLYMORE CASTLE, Co. WESTMEATH

A Sergeant and fifteen Men being in an old Castle nigh a quarter of a Mile to the South West of the Fort, after all hopes of being relieved, was cut off; the Sergeant fired upon some of our Men and killed one or two, for which, as soon as the Castle was Surrendered, he was hanged.

These are the words of the Reverend George Story, author of the self-styled *Impartial History of the Wars in Ireland* (1693), in describing a castle near the fort of Ballymore, which formed almost an island on the southern shores of Lough Sewdy (or Sunderlin) in the county of Westmeath.

On his map, to the east of the lake, Story marks what seems like a tower on top of a hill marked 'The Irish Sergeant's hill'. But the tower shown opposite, in Cooper's copy of a drawing by his cousin Samuel Walker, is the one that lies to the south-west of the lakeside fort. Thus, I believe we may take this round castle – which is marked as such on Story's maps – to have been the one from which

the Sergeant shot, and got himself hanged for his trouble.

All of these bloodthirsty acts took place on 7 June 1691, when the Williamite army under Ginckel was moving westwards towards Athlone. The Irish had taken 1000 men from Athlone to entrench themselves beside Lough Sewdy, in an existing fort. 'Firing their small Shot, and two small Turkish Pieces that were mounted upon old Cart-Wheels', the Irish, despite their numbers, had little chance of successfully defending their positions and, within two days, were forced to surrender. Ginckel and his company went on to Athlone, Aughrim and Limerick with the direst consequences for Ireland, which still have echoes down to our own day.

Eddie Geraghty, the present owner of the castle, told me of a local tradition that claims Ginckel blew the roof off and, even in Cooper's day, the signs of battering can be seen in the first-floor window visible in the drawing opposite. In 1991, the sad events of 1691 were recreated in a tercentenary commemoration – but this time, fortunately, without any loss of life.

S. Walker delin.t   A.C. pinxt 9.º April 1792

Castle of **Ballymore** — Co.ª *Westmeath* —

NORTH GATE, ATHLONE, Co. WESTMEATH

The North Gate at Athlone no longer exists – only its memory is perpetuated in the name Northgate Street, where it stood at the corner of Lucas Lane. It was certainly an imposing fortification, and a stern deterrent to anyone who might have wanted to enter the town illicitly. It was one of only two gates that gave access to the eastern half of Athlone, on the Dublin side of the Shannon. In addition, it guarded the approach of those coming southwards from the eastern side of Lough Ree, and provided protection against any boats that might have considered making a sudden attack downstream along the Shannon.

Except for the archway at ground level, the gate could easily be mistaken for a tower house, with its squat proportions, crenellations at parapet level and small windows for defence. What Cooper shows us or, to be more exact, what Samuel Walker showed in his original drawing, which was copied by Cooper, is the outside of the tower, and the dark patch at the bottom is the River Shannon lapping up against the tower's portal.

Any visitor approaching from outside could not fail to have been impressed by the plaque inserted above the arch, which bore the arms of Elizabeth I – 'England and France only, supported by a lion and a griffin', as Harman Murtagh discovered from the account of an eighteenth-century traveller. The gate probably predates 1578, when one Robert Damport, provost-marshal of Connacht, lived there, having come to Athlone a decade earlier to oversee the construction of the Shannon bridge.

Even down to the small one-roomed building next to it, the gate looked much the same when George Petrie made his sketch of it for Vol. II of Cromwell's *Excursions Through Ireland*, published in 1820. This state of affairs was not to last as the gate appears to have been swept away sometime around 1840, probably in the course of urban expansion.

S. Walker delin.   J.C. pinxt.

10.ᵗ April 1792

North Gate *at* Athlone

KILCONNELL CROSS, Co. GALWAY

The village of Kilconnell in Co. Galway is best known for its Franciscan friary, a fine fifteenth-century example of the genre, with a tall, central tower and a number of good funerary monuments of the later medieval period. But in the centre of the village, at the junction of the New Inn, Kiltullagh and Loughrea roads, there is a cross dating from the seventeenth century – a period during which at least a hundred stone crosses were erected in Ireland, many of them requesting a prayer from the passing traveller.

Writing in the *Journal of Post-Medieval Archaeology* in 1985, Heather King – one of the few who has devoted any attention to these crosses in recent years – pointed out that their greatest concentration was in Leinster, and that there were only just over a dozen crosses erected west of the Shannon, thus making the Kilconnell cross something of a rarity. At present, it stands on a square base, which is obviously a modern replacement for the stepped one shown in Cooper's drawing. The shaft too, when compared with that of Cooper's 1792 sketch, is also modern. Even the cross on top is different to that shown by Cooper, which has much more extended arms, and an illegible carving (possibly two

letters) at the bottom of the uppermost limb. This leaves us with the 'bulbous collar' of the cross, which is genuine and original. It bears an inscription in raised lettering:

Orate pro D. Ioane Donellano
Eiusque Familia Qui Hanc A.D.
Crucem Erigi Fecit 1682

which in translation reads as:

A prayer for John Donellan and his family,
who had this cross erected in 1682

A subsequent inscription proclaims that the cross was re-erected by the parish priest of Kilconnell, the Reverend W Manning, in 1844.

John O'Donovan, in his *Tribes and Customs of Hy-Many* (1843), noted that the tradition in the county was that the cross would bow whenever any of the Bally-Donellan family pass to be buried. Perhaps it was a surfeit of Donellan funerals that caused it to topple between the time Cooper drew it and when Fr Manning re-erected it some sixty years later!

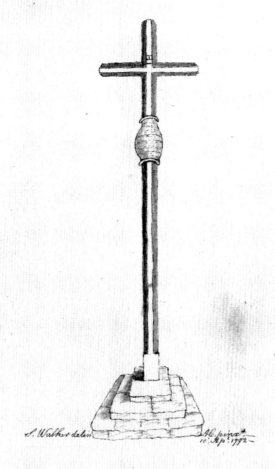

S. Walker delin.   *AC. pinxt.*
10. Ap: 1792 —

Cross at **Kilconnel** Co:y Galway

Inscription on the Ball —

IHS Orate pro D. Joanno Donellano qui hanc ejusque familia crucem erigi fecit —
1682 —

LYNCH HOUSE, GALWAY

The story is told in Galway that a mayor of the city, John Lynch, hanged his own son in 1493, because the boy had committed a murder, and no one else was prepared to carry out the sentence. The tale has wrongly been used to explain the origin of the phrase 'Lynch law', but it is probably wrong itself. In the *Journal of the Galway Archaeological and Historical Society for 1966–1971*, James Mitchell shows it to be largely a romantic fiction less than two centuries old, invented or embellished by Hardiman, the author of a *History of Galway* in 1820.

The event is said to have taken place at the back of a house in Lombard Street, near the church of St Nicholas, and Hardiman said that the front window of this same house was distinguished by a handsome representation, carved in black marble, of a human skull with two bones crossed beneath. It is dated 1624, and is supposed to have been put up by some of the Lynch family as a public memorial. In a miscellaneous plate, Hardiman illustrated the plaque, giving as its motto 'Remember Deathe/Vaniti of Vaniti & all is but Vaniti'.

This must surely be the same plaque shown opposite in Cooper's copy of his cousin Samuel Walker's original, and the same that was placed above one side of the front door on what the caption says is 'Lynch's House in Lombard Street – Galway'. The problem is that the building illustrated by Hardiman is so different to that shown here that one must ask whether they are two different buildings, or whether the Lynch house illustrated here got a facelift so severe as to make it look like that depicted by Hardiman.

However, the 'Cooper version' looks like a genuine late medieval townhouse of the kind best represented in Galway city by Lynch's Castle, and it is probably the oldest detailed picture we have of Lynch's house. This was apparently demolished in 1840, but the stone with the inscribed skull and cross-bones was preserved and built as a temporary measure into a wall that was meant to look like the demolished house. The longer it lasted, the more it (unintentionally) fooled people into thinking that it really was the old Lynch house. The charade became even more moving in 1978 when stone and 'house' were re-sited in Market Street, an extension of Lombard Street, where the stone is built in over a blocked up doorway that at least looks much closer to that in Cooper's drawing than anything in Hardiman's illustration.

REMEMBER DEATHE
VANITI OF VANITI
ALIS BUT VANITI

Over the Door

S. Walker delin.

AC pinx 11 Ap. 1792

Lynch's House in Lombard Street   Galway

FORE ABBEY, Co. WESTMEATH

For almost a millennium and a half, the Benedictines have been one of the greatest religious Orders in Europe. Yet, curiously, their foundations in Ireland have been fewer in number than those of other Orders that came to Ireland from Europe after the religious reforms of the twelfth century.

The Benedictines' first Irish house was founded on the Rock of Cashel in the 1130s. Gwynn and Hadcock, the authors of *Medieval Religious Houses, Ireland* (1970), suggest that their church was what we know today as Cormac's Chapel. Unfortunately, between 1269 and 1272, they were driven out by David MacCarvill, the archbishop of Cashel, because he had had a dream that they were going to cut off his head! He replaced them with Cistercian monks for whom he founded Hore Abbey (nos.8 and 9).

Rather more permanent was the Benedictine foundation at Fore in Co. Westmeath, with the monastery set in a lovely oasis-like valley, which still evokes the seven wonders associated with St Fechín, who had founded an earlier monastery there in the seventh century. This abbey was founded by the powerful baron Hugh de Lacy, who granted it to the abbey of St Taurin, at Evreux in northern France. This was a circumstance that came back to haunt Fore during the Hundred Years War between France and England in the fourteenth century, when the English monarchs repeatedly seized the monastery as an alien priory.

The monastic buildings form an impressive complex nestling in the small, unexpected hills of Co. Westmeath. But, as the drawing shows, lurking at either end of the church are towers, thick and thin, which suggest that, as an Irish Benedictine enclave affiliated to a French mother house, it always needed to be on its guard. Nevertheless, Fore is the only medieval Benedictine monastery in Ireland whose actual physical remains survive to the present day. Those remains indicate a rather austere building, relieved only by a few decorative features, such as the three lancet windows in the east gable seen here. The original drawing that Cooper has copied was done by a Mr Monk – sadly his name is the extent of our knowledge about the artist.

Mr. Monk delin.

Ab. print 3 Nov. 1799

E View of Fore – Co. Westmeath

NEWCASTLE, Co. LIMERICK

This castle is surely one of the most noticeable antiquities for the traveller coming out from Limerick on the Nenagh–Dublin road, as it stands gauntly against the skyline on a notable bluff on the right-hand side about two miles from the city. It would probably be reckoned as belonging nowadays to Castletroy, which is located on the banks of the Shannon between Plassey and Annacotty. By a curious coincidence, Castletroy Castle was also illustrated in Cooper's album in the National Library – but by a different hand.

Newcastle, in the Cooper drawing, which he copies from an original executed by his cousin Samuel Walker, is a five-storey building with notable gables surmounted by tall chimney-stacks, dating it to the reign of Elizabeth I (1558–1603). TJ Westropp, an archaeologist who made a very useful collection of historical references to the castles of Co. Limerick, notes that the name is given as 'Castlenou' in 1583, which might indicate that it had not been long built at that stage (although the name 'new' has a funny habit of sticking to an object long after its novelty value has worn off!).

The castle passed through many hands, including, in the seventeenth century, those of the Duke of York (later James II), and the speculators known as the Hollow Sword Blades Company.

Viewed from the Limerick side, the whole of the western gable is missing, having collapsed around 1800. But a drawing in the seventeenth-century Down Survey shows the building had crenellations and a very tall roof – the former not easy to reconcile with the chimneyed gables seen in Cooper's drawing.

Castle of New Castle — Co.ᵈ Limerick

2 Miles from Limerick on the Dublin Road

S. Walker delin.

A 6 pinxᵗ
14ᵗʰ April 1792

ST CRONAN'S CROSS, ROSCREA, Co. TIPPERARY

Until recently, when it was removed for repairs, St Cronan's Cross stood just a few yards south of the façade of a church dedicated to the same seventh-century local saint (see no.63). It is generally believed that St Cronan is the figure represented on the head of the cross shown here, standing and holding his (now headless) crozier in front of him. The folds of the lower part of his garment were much clearer in Cooper's day than they are now.

Figures of abbots or bishops appear on a number of twelfth-century Irish High Crosses – one thinks of Cashel, Dysert O'Dea, Kilfenora and Tuam – and they are normally taken to be a product of the church reform movement, which swept Ireland during the twelfth century. Of all of the crosses surviving from that period, St Cronan's at Roscrea is likely to have been one of the finest, but the weathering of the stone has given it a rather pitted surface, which does not give us a true picture of its former quality.

Samuel Walker's picture, as copied by Cooper, over-emphasises the length of the surviving arms, and a simple segment of an arc with a small 'nodule' on the inside is here turned into a shape that resembles an archer's bow. Not unique, but nevertheless unusual among the twelfth-century crosses, is the stepped pattern on the shaft and arms, which may have been derived from carpentry or metalwork forms.

The shaft, shown here beside the head, is divided into a number of panels on the broad side shown in shadow. The two figures clearly visible on the lowest panels represent Adam and Eve, and there are animals interlaced in the panels above. The side of the cross might also appear at first sight to be divided up into two panels, separated by a bar at about the same level as that above Adam and Eve on the broad face. But this, in fact, is a tall, thin – and unidentified – figure, standing out in relief from the side of the cross.

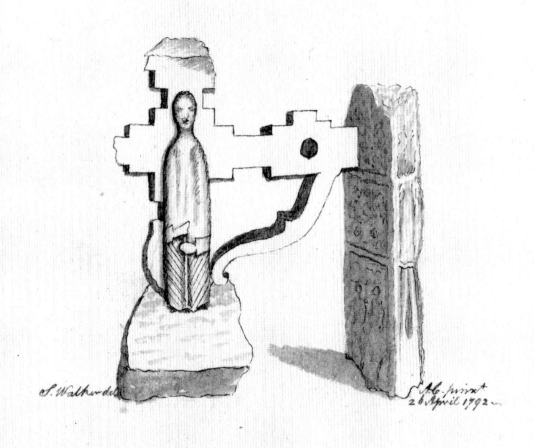

S. Walker del.   *AC pinxt*
26 April 1792

Parts of St Cronan Cross at Roscrea

OLD CASTLE AT MARYBORO/PORTLAOISE, Co. LAOIS

Samuel Walker's drawing copied, as before, by his cousin Austin Cooper, shows part of the castle at Maryboro – now Portlaoise, Co. Laois – which started off its life in 1548 as Fort Protector. This was at the start of the short reign of Edward VI, the youthful son and successor of Henry VIII who had attempted, with limited success, to make all of the inhabitants of Ireland his subjects, and had begun to extend the Pale beyond its narrow limits around Dublin.

Ireland's Lord Deputy, a man named Bellingham, initiated work on the fort, which was a broad rectangle in shape. The rounded bastion on the northern corner survives, flanked by some of the original walls of the fort. The roughly square tower at the opposite southern corner no longer exists, but the drawing reproduced opposite presumably shows part of that tower, topped by a small, rounded turret, which is seen in greater detail in an engraving in Grose's *Antiquities of Ireland.*

Its former location at the back of the present Vocational School was pointed out to me by the local historian, Michael Parsons, who suggested that the fort may have acted as a model for later military settlements in Virginia, USA. The fort was garrisoned by more than a hundred men, and was given a new name, Maryborough, in 1557, after the English queen, Mary I.

In Paul Kerrigan's very useful 1995 volume *Castles and Fortifications in Ireland 1485–1945*, there is a very interesting map of the castle, dating from 1571. It shows how the castle – which had been given the added protection of earthen ramparts – was now surrounded on three sides by an urban settlement, itself protected by another rampart or wall, which was part of the larger-scale plantation of the Queen's County, as Laois was then called.

After the end of the Elizabethan wars, the castle became the centre of a garrison town, which, in 1650, was taken from the Confederates by the Cromwellian generals Reynolds and Hewson. They levelled most of the fort, leaving what little survives today and what was shown in Cooper's drawing and Grose's engraving – both, by curious coincidence, executed independently of one another in the same year, 1793.

S. Walker delin.   AC. pinx 29. March 1793

Old Castle at **Maryboro'**, Queen's Co.

KILLENURE CASTLE, Co. TIPPERARY

The subject of the drawing opposite must have had a special place in Austin Cooper's heart: Killenure was not only his birthplace, but had been the family home since 1746, thirteen years before he was born.

It was presumably in the house on the right that Cooper first saw the light of day, the castle on the left having been a ruin long before he came into the world. Its remains certainly indicate a once-fine building, consisting of a central rectangular block with a circular tower at each corner. This is a typically Irish ground-plan, with an ancestry that goes back to the early thirteenth century at places such as Carlow (no.37), and continuing into the fifteenth and sixteenth centuries at Dunmoe (no.129) and Enniscorthy in Co. Wexford. Killenure Castle must be one of the latest examples, as it probably dates to the reign of Elizabeth I sometime in the last years of the sixteenth century. Its forest of chimneys supports such a date, and the string courses above the ground and second floors give it an elegance unusual in other Irish castles.

The castle was, apparently, built by the O'Dwyer family and, having been burned by Cromwell's troops, the property was used by the Coppingers as a hunting 'box' before the Coopers bought it. It may well have been Austin's father William who built the two-storey cottage over the basement, as seen in the drawing. This, presumably, was the house that Austin left when he departed for Dublin at the age of 15 to become a clerk in the Treasury.

The family stayed on here for another six generations, changing the house during the course of the nineteenth century, including one major alteration whereby the entrance door was turned ninety degrees and inserted into the south-facing niche wall. The old house was incorporated into the new building, which was extended towards the castle, so that one of the castle's bastions was actually restored to become an extra – and romantic – bedroom.

But the Coopers finally had to leave the castle in the 1960s, and it was sold by the Land Commission in 1967. Turned into a small private school by its next owners, the Baileys, it subsequently came into the possession of its present owner, Mrs Roth, in 1984. She keeps up the house in a style of which the former Cooper owners would undoubtedly have been proud.

ST MARY'S CHURCH, INISHMURRAY, Co. SLIGO

Inishmurray or, as Cooper calls it, Ennismurry, is an island about four miles off the coast of Co. Sligo, usually accessible by boat from Mullaghmore. It is one of those islands that retains a kind of mystique – once there were people living there, but it has now been deserted for more than half a century. However, the houses of the former inhabitants are still standing, though in most cases the roofs have caved in.

Other than the adventure of landing on an Atlantic island, what attracts people to Inishmurray is the well-preserved early Christian settlement – and this, indeed, is what brought Gabriel Beranger there in the summer of 1779 along with his Italian friend and fellow artist Angelo Maria Bigari. The pair had been commissioned by William Burton (later Conyngham) of Slane Castle to do a tour of Ulster and Connacht.

The purpose of the tour was to create a collection of drawings of the antiquities in those regions. These, it was hoped, would eventually appear in one or a number of volumes intended to show the beauty of Irish antiquities, as Grose and others had already done for British monuments. Alas, it was not to be; some of the architectural drawings as copied here by Cooper do not survive in any other form, and represent, therefore, a unique record of this early Christian complex as it was more than 220 years ago.

The main focus on the island is the oval cashel, or enclosing wall. One of the structures within is the 'cell', illustrated opposite, which would be described in modern parlance as 'a beehive hut'. It is half hidden in the earth and stones have accumulated around it to just below window level. Well built, albeit without mortar, its name in Irish is Toorybhrenell, which might suggest that it was associated with the cult of St Brendan – as is another less complete hut bearing a similar name on the island of Inishglora, off the Mayo coast.

The window, top right, is the east window of a nearby church known as Teampall Molaise, a church named after the founding father, Molaise, who may have lived in the sixth century. But the church itself may be 500 years later – the round-arched window gives the impression of an eleventh- or twelfth-century date, though, if this be the case, it is curious that there is not a single trace of any Romanesque decoration surviving on the island.

One church outside the cashel, St Mary's, otherwise known as Teampall na mBan, or the Ladies' Church, is shown here in plan. The fact that it is dedicated to the Virgin and has a doorway in the south wall prompts the suggestion that this church may belong to the later medieval period.

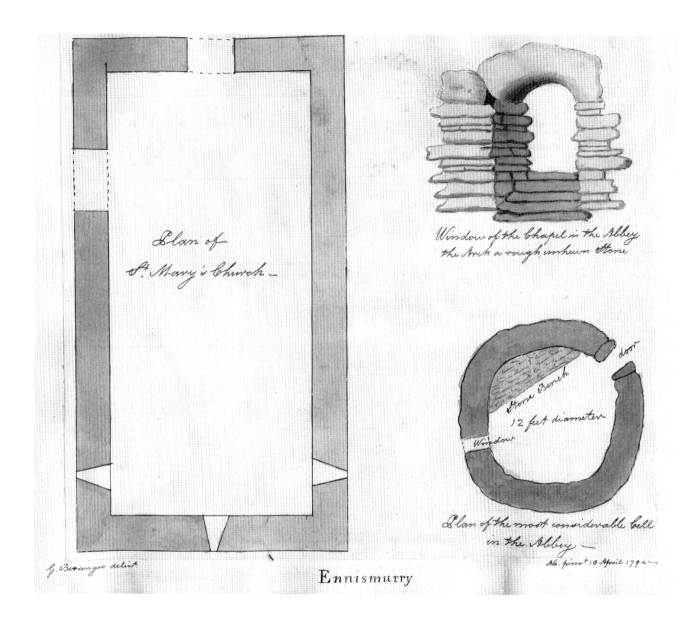

Plan of
St. Mary's Church —

G. Beranger delint

Ennismurry

Window of the Chapel in the Abbey
the Arch a rough unhewn Stone

Stone Bench

door

12 feet diameter

Window

Plan of the most considerable Cell
in the Abbey —

AB. pinxt 18 April 1794

243

ANTIQUITIES ON INISHMURRAY, Co. SLIGO

Cooper packed a lot on to this page, probably copying in detail a sheet done by Beranger in the summer of 1779, when he visited the island with his artist friend, Bigari, and his Sligo host, Lewis Irwin of Tanrego House. For his tenants, Irwin brought supplies of food and drink, and all the grown-up ladies on the island lined up beside the landing place to be kissed one by one by the three men on arrival – a ceremony conducted in reverse before the party left the island three days later! On the left of the drawing is the great pilgrimage station of the Trinity, a walled enclosure containing a rectangular altar, upon which stands an upright slab with cross decoration that does not appear in Cooper's copy of Beranger's drawing.

In the centre, top and bottom, is what is probably the oldest and certainly the most venerable of all the monuments on Inishmurray. This is St Molaise's House, a reliquary shrine wherein is buried the founding saint, Molaise. Recent radio-carbon dating suggests that it could be from the ninth century, and it is unusual in having a stone roof, which has been much repaired and altered over the years.

On the plan, the 'place of the statue' is marked by two feet shown on a small ledge that goes around two sides of the interior. The statue in question is the wooden statue (right) of St Molaise, dating from around the thirteenth century, which was revered on the island before it was brought to the National Museum in Dublin after the island was finally abandoned in 1948. The statue was certainly movable long before that: in an illustration from *The Protestant Penny Magazine* of 1834, the editor has drawn the statue – which he calls 'Father Molagh' here – in the other corner, beside the window. He describes it as a 'melancholy-visaged idol', which he was horrified to note received the adoration of his coun-trymen on this island celebrated for its superstitions! For all that, an Irish wooden statue surviving from the thirteenth century is a great rarity.

Finally, on the far right are the cursing stones, a set of rounded and sometimes decorated stones, which can be turned against an individual who has done evil in order to right a wrong. Should the accusation turn out to be unjust, however, the curse can rebound back on whoever turns the stone. The Protestant editor mentioned above remarked that the islanders felt that the stones were particularly efficacious on one occasion, when they had been turned on members of the coast-guard – all of whom were drowned a short time later.

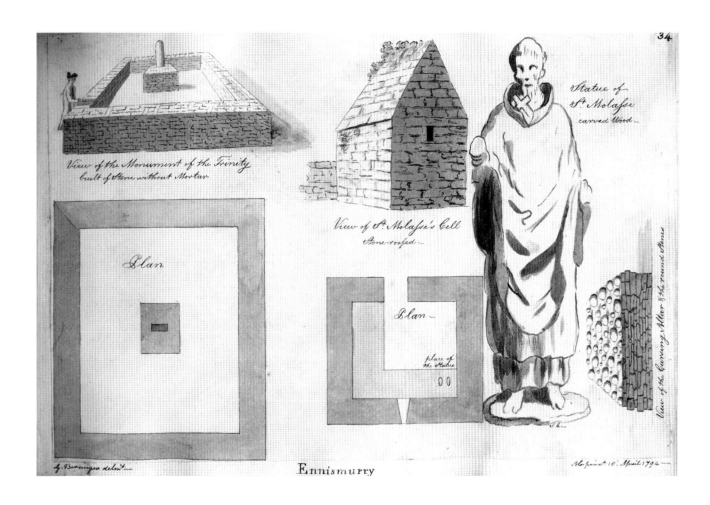

View of the Monument of the Trinity
built of Stone without Mortar.

Plan

View of S.t Molasse's Cell
Stone-roofed.

Plan

place of
the Statue

Statue of
S.t Molasse
carved Wood.

View of the Carving Altar & the round Stone

G. Beranger delin.t

Ennismurry

blue print 18.t April 1794

PLAN OF INISHMURRAY, CO. SLIGO

The plan of the cashel, or *caiseal*, on the island of Inishmurray off the Sligo coast, was drawn by Gabriel Beranger in 1779 and copied in the drawing opposite by Austin Cooper in 1794. It was the first one ever published, because it was used – without acknowledgement of authorship – by Edward Ledwich in Grose's *Antiquities of Ireland*. Ledwich changed the letters around somewhat but his plan is, in essence, the same as Beranger's. It is all the more valuable because it is the only plan known to have been executed before the Board of Works 'restorations' of a century later, the details of which went sadly unrecorded. The only other illustration we have prior to the nineteenth-century restoration are the photographs in the earl of Dunraven's *Notes on Irish Architecture* of 1875.

The building which Beranger marks as A is known as Teampall Molaise, whose walls were raised considerably in the Board of Works reconstruction. The building marked B is Teampall na Teinidh, a later medieval church that gets its name from a fire which is said to have burned on the floor. This was an ancient custom, reminiscent of the fire-house in St Brigid's Monastery in Kildare (no.60). This building was removed by the Board of Works.

Teach Molaise, or St Molaise's House, already encountered on the previous page, is a reliquary shrine that goes back, perhaps, as far as the ninth century. It has been much altered down the years, the plank shuttering on the interior roof probably being one of the more necessary repairs carried out by the Board of Works.

Beranger marks a number of 'cells', one of which, bearing the letter F, is now an integral part of the wall of the Cashel. The others are in a raised area roughly east to south-east of the church marked B (the Beranger/Cooper plan is orientated somewhat east of south). The D on the right is Toorybhrenell (mentioned in no.114), otherwise known as the Schoolhouse, having been used for this purpose in the nineteenth century.

One of the interesting features of this plan is the way the other two cells, E and the second D, are emphasised. These cells are not clear on the detailed maps published by Wakeman in 1893, but the suggestion is that excavation of the area might reveal the presence of more beehive huts than are known at present. For Edward Ledwich, 'in these cells the Firbolgian priests resided, and they were succeeded in them by Christian Asceticks' – to which, even if one doesn't believe it all, may probably be added 'pilgrims' and the usual inhabitants of the island. What tantalisingly little we know about this early monastery, has been gathered together in the only book written by one of the islanders, Dr Patrick Heraughty's *Inishmurray, Ancient Monastic Island*, published first in 1982 and recently re-issued.

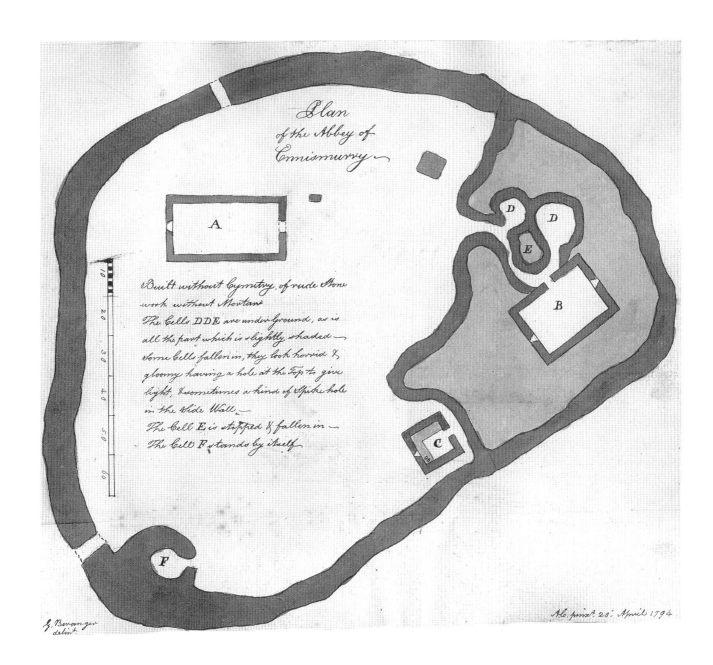

Plan
of the Abbey of
Ennismurry.

A

Built without Cymetry, of rude Stone
work without Mortar.
The Cells DDE are under Ground, as is
all the part which is slightly shaded.
some Cells fallen in, they look horrid &
gloomy having a hole at the Top to give
light, & sometimes a kind of Spike hole
in the Side Wall.
The Cell E is stopped & fallen in.
The Cell F stands by itself.

D
D
E
B
C
F

10
20
30
40
50
60

G. Bevanger
delint.

A.C. pinxt. 20: April 1794.

247

BANADA ABBEY, Co. SLIGO

The same tour of Connacht that brought Gabriel Beranger and Angelo Maria Bigari to Inishmurray, Co. Sligo, also brought them to another monument in the same county – a place that is now largely forgotten, due to the destruction and decay that has taken place since their visit in 1779. Their drawings were copied years later by Cooper who called this place the 'Abbey of Banada', although it should be labelled more correctly a friary, since it was founded in 1423 as a house of the Augustinian friars rather than the canons of the same Order. Banada is in the west of Sligo, not far from the Mayo border, and just a few miles south of the Tubbercurry–Ballina road.

Cooper's copy was rather hastily done, as the tree on the right demonstrates. We get a much better idea of the quality of the original drawing if we compare Cooper's sketch with the engraving of the same subject in Grose's *Antiquities of Ireland,* which was enlivened with the addition of a family – father, mother and son – standing just beyond the arch.

The original drawing – preserved in the National Library as p.13 of manuscript 2122 TX (3) and reproduced by Anne Crookshank and the Knight of Glin on p.41 of *The Watercolours of Ireland* (1994) – shows a funeral scene with more vigorous activity. One man fills in a grave, another carries to it a tombstone on his back, while the well-dressed women of the family weep and keen, and the men discuss weighty matters.

The drawing gives the impression that the tower and church walls are made up of large ashlar blocks, but this is more a reflection of Bigari's style in drawing Irish masonry than of the true character of the stonework itself. But, at least as far as the tower is concerned, we will never know the character of its craftsmanship because the 70ft-high tower fell on 21 November 1897. It had, apparently, been undermined by the removal of large blocks for use as tombstones, as Maire McDonnell-Garvey, the friary's most recent historian, tells us in *The Corran Herald* for 1999/2000. The tower itself may have been a mid-fifteenth-century addition that benefited from an indulgence granted in 1444–45.

Cooper's detailed drawing of the ogee-headed windows of the tower, seen opposite on the top right, seems to be his own inspiration, since it does not feature in Bigari's original.

One intriguing mystery in the drawing is the presence of a head, apparently acting as a pillar capital in a chapel off the south aisle. No trace of this head survives where it stood, and it seems unlikely that it is identical with the head that is built into the existing north wall of the choir – probably part of the fifteenth-century effigy of a lady.

Abbey of Bennada _ Co. Sligo

PLAN OF BANADA ABBEY, CO. SLIGO

The Augustinian canons arrived in Ireland even before the Cistercians in the first half of the twelfth century. They had numerous houses, many of them large and with considerable variations in the cloister buildings usually attached to them, as illustrated in a very useful large-scale comparison in Tadhg O'Keeffe's book on Bridgetown, Co. Cork, entitled *An Anglo-Norman Monastery* (1999).

But our information about the architecture of that other branch of the same Order – the Augustinian or Austin friars – is much more sketchy since very few of their churches, let alone their cloisters, have managed to survive to our own day. It is all the more gratifying, therefore, to have here the plan of the friary at Banada, particularly as little or nothing remains of the cloister buildings today.

The church itself was divided into two unequal parts by the tower, whose two supporting walls can be seen here jutting towards one another from the north and south walls respectively. The north side of the nave was widened to incorporate an aisle, separated from the nave by an arcade indicated on the plan by circular pillars. The main entrance was, curiously, at the western end of the aisle rather than in the nave, as is usually the case. At the eastern end of the aisle there is a transept chapel, the west wall of which, unusually, is attached to one of the arcade pillars.

The nave had a traceried window in the east gable and, near it at the eastern end of the south wall, a doorway and sedilia, which are illustrated overleaf. The door once led to the cloister buildings shown here on the right-hand side, of which, sadly, little remains.

The gable of what may have been the sacristy (though not directly connected to the church by a doorway) is seen in Bigari's original drawing of the church, already referred to previously as being preserved in the National Library. However, Cocking's view of the friary from the south-east, engraved for Grose's *Antiquities*, does not show any gable. But it does illustrate a two-light window at the eastern end of the south wall, near to the altar – which is not indicated on the plan.

Cocking places the friary in a beautiful raised landscape, with the River Moy flowing at its foot. The friars must have been able to pull out many a salmon from it before Henry VIII dissolved their foundation at the time of the Reformation.

Cooper copied this plan from an original drawing by Gabriel Beranger, now preserved on p.35 in the National Library's manuscript 2122 TX (3).

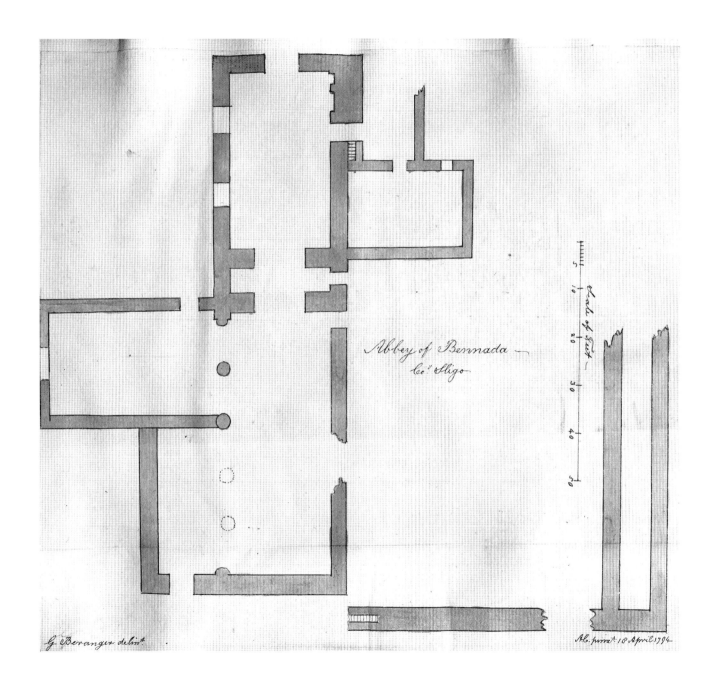

Abbey of Bennada
Co. Sligo

G. Beranger delint.

Al. pinxt 18 April 1794

x

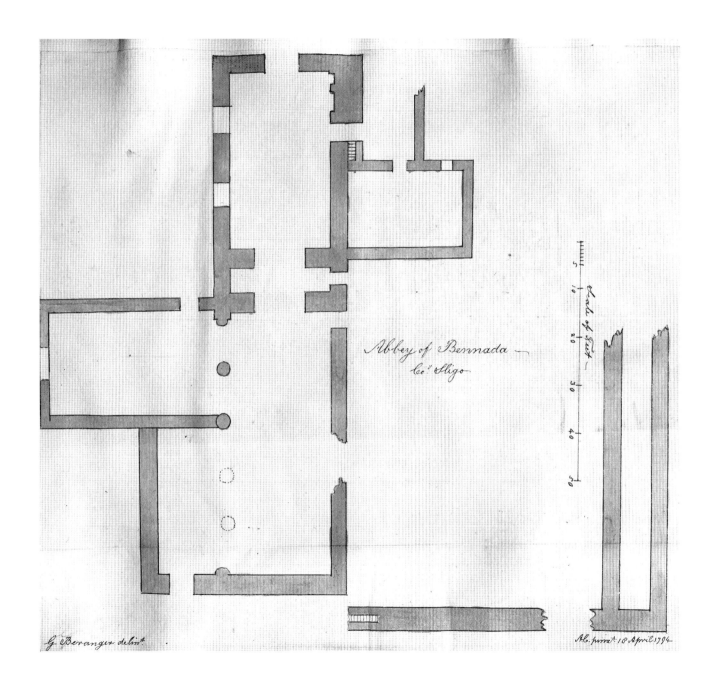

Abbey of Bennada
Co. Sligo

Scale of Feet
5 10 20 30 40 50

G. Beranger delint.

Al. pinxt 18 April 1794

251

DETAILS OF BANADA ABBEY, CO. SLIGO

The same sheet (National Library manuscript 2122 TX (3) p.35) that preserved Gabriel Beranger's original plan of Banada Abbey in Co. Sligo, also contains his drawings of architectural details, which Austin Cooper copied as well – probably in 1794, though he does not actually provide a date.

What we can see on the upper left is part of what is called the 'Monument', perhaps a three-cusped tomb niche with a hood moulding, narrowing to a knot, that loops again before blossoming out into three leaves. Now sadly disappeared, this might have been part of one of those 'two handsome ancient tombs in the church' to which Grose's *Antiquities* refers.

On the right is a traceried window with quatrefoil decoration, which presumably once decorated the east gable of the church and of which, again, not a trace remains.

In the middle drawing we see not a 'Monument' as Beranger/Cooper called it, but the fine remains of a sedilia – a set of arched seats in the south wall near the altar, which were built to provide comfort for the celebrants at Mass. Despite a large tree growing near it, this can still be appreciated as a very fine example of its kind in medieval Ireland – having a fluted pillar on one side with base and capital bearing mouldings similar to those shown on the 'Monument' beside it. It is probably more than a coincidence that one of the finest Irish sedilia, according to HG Leask, was in the friary

at Callan, Co. Kilkenny (no.70), which was also an Augustinian, or Austin, house. This decorative feature may, therefore, have been a speciality of theirs, although Callan is a later foundation than Banada by almost forty years.

The Augustinian friars were leaders in the Observantine reform of the fifteenth century. This was a movement among the different Orders – including Franciscans and Dominicans – to get back to a stricter observance of their monastic rule. The spiritual leadership associated with the Observantines made it into one of the liveliest religious movements of the later medieval period.

Banada itself was not a case of conventional friars converting to Observantine practice – it was founded specifically by the O'Haras for the Observantines, the first instance of its kind among the Irish Augustinians, and indeed one of the earliest Irish Observantine houses of any of the mendicant Orders. The Dominicans had started earlier, but Banada was more dynamic in helping the movement to spread to other parts of Ireland. The recently deceased historian, FX Martin, considered that it was the Observantine movement that ensured the survival of the Augustinians' in Ireland. In fact, seven years after Callan became Observantine, it became the Order's main house in following the Observantine reform movement in Ireland.

Monument   Monument   Window

4 feet

The Whole   5 feet

2 feet 4 inches

Door

Bennada – Co: Sligo

41

TAGHADOE CHURCH AND TOWER, Co. KILDARE

Taghadoe is one of Leinster's least-known Round Towers, as it lies off the beaten track some two and a half miles south-south-west of Maynooth. Cooper copied his drawing, opposite, from an original by one Pope Stevens Reilly, one of a family of amateur and professional painters, whose artistic identities are difficult to unravel. Pope Stevens Reilly is also known to have worked in Co. Wicklow, and was probably counted among the circle of friends of William Burton (later Conyngham) of Slane Castle.

In this drawing, Stevens Reilly shows the tower from the south-west, with a gaping hole at ground level that allowed the tower to be used for storing coal during the nineteenth century, until the Board of Works blocked it up when the tower was declared a National Monument in 1886. The real door was on the other side; it is round headed with a raised architrave accentuating its outline. On the stone immediately above there is a bump, which could be a worn human head, or even part of a Crucified Christ like the one Cooper drew at Donaghmore in the neighbouring county of Meath (no.123).

The reason Stevens Reilly chose not to draw the side with the door in it was presumably in order to show the church, though it seems to have had little to recommend it other than a rounded doorway in the west gable. It was demolished to make way for a replacement erected with a grant from the Board of First Fruits in the year 1831 – itself now a ruin, and a National Monument to boot. According to the *Parliamentary Gazetteer*, the number attending church services was fifteen in 1846, when the parish of Taghadoe consisted of four churchmen, three Protestant dissenters – and 470 Roman Catholics.

Pope Stevens Reilly delint   AC Pim 17 Oct. 1794

Church & Tower of **Teghadow** Co. Kildare

KILLALA ROUND TOWER, Co. MAYO

Here, once more, it is Gabriel Beranger who provided the raw material for Cooper to copy into his album in 1794. The original drawing was executed in 1779, when Beranger and his Italian friend Bigari were on a tour of Connacht, making sketches of antiquities for Colonel William Burton (later Conyngham) of Slane Castle.

Through his Mayo host, a man named Colonel Cuffe, Beranger was introduced to Bishop Hutchinson of Killala, and he went to see the Round Tower at Killala with the bishop's two sons. Here he drew not only the tower but also the skull of a whale, which had been washed onto the shore nearby. It was then that Beranger worked out the height of the tower to be 84ft. This statistic has generally been followed by later artists and writers, who have found it difficult to take accurate measurements, because of the presence of modern houses around the limestone bluff on which the tower stands. The artist also got out his measuring tape and worked out the circumference of the tower to be 51ft, and the width of the wall – presumably at the level of the doorway – to be 3½ft.

Beranger gives a drawing of the doorway, which is picked out in sandstone from the remainder of the limestone masonry. The lower part of the tower contains some large Cyclopean blocks, and the drawing shows a large gap in the masonry caused by lightning. This was repaired in 1841 by the Dean, who was probably also responsible for having restored the top of the conical cap shown as defective in the drawing.

The Round Tower doubtless formed part of an early medieval monastery. Little is known of its history, but local tradition says that St Patrick left a bishop named Muiredach here to look after the fledgling Christian community. The monastery's area was probably extensive, and the Church of Ireland cathedral, some 200ft away, may stand on the site of the original church of the monastery. Unusual in having a plinth or offset at its base, this Round Tower is undoubtedly one of the best-preserved examples of the genre, and still dominates the town nestling at its foot.

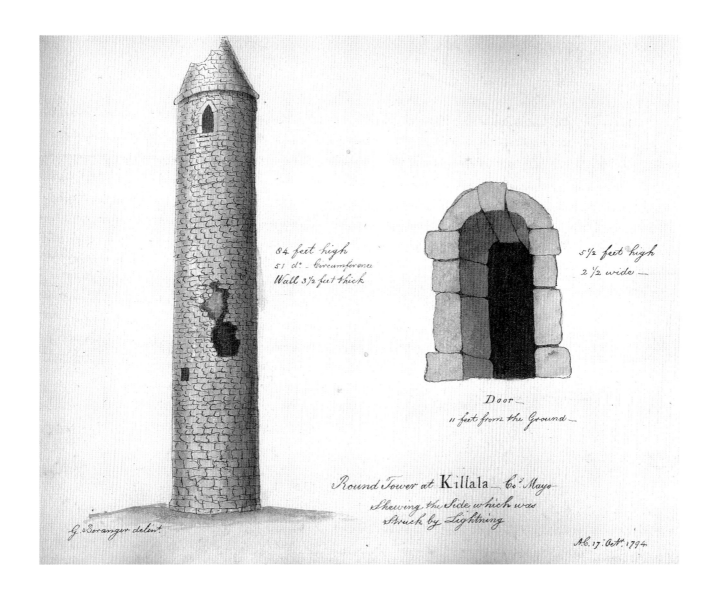

84 feet high
51 d.º Circumference
Wall 3½ feet thick

5½ feet high
2½ wide

Door
11 feet from the Ground

Round Tower at Killala Co. Mayo
Shewing the Side which was
Struck by Lightning

G. Beranger delin.t

A.C. 17.º Oct.r 1794

DONAGHMORE CHURCH AND TOWER, Co. MEATH

Written in an anonymous hand – probably that of Cooper's grandson, Austin Damer Cooper – the following description adorns the page opposite the drawing of the 'Church and Tower of Donoghmore, Co Meath':

> Adjoining the demesne of Black Castle, on the Slane road, about a mile from Navan, on the western bank of the river, we pass through the group of ecclesiastical ruins figured in the drawing – the Round Tower and church of Donoghmore. The original church, called Domnach-mor-muighe Echnach, i.e. the great church of the plain of Echnach, is said to owe its origin to St Patrick. The very beautiful Round Tower is built of limestone undressed, except around the doorway and other apertures, and is of admirable masonry. It has two projecting ledges or steps at its base, and six rests for others. The circumference of the tower near its base, is 66 feet 6 inches, and its height about 100 feet. The wall is 3 feet thick, and the doorway 12 feet from the ground, and is 5 feet 2 inches high. It is 2 feet 3 inches wide at the bottom, and 2 feet beneath the spring of the arch at top. It is supposed to have been built about the 9th or 10th century, and agrees in architectural style and mason work with that of Kells, which was founded by St Columbkill in the 6th century.

With the exception of the last statement (Kells was probably not founded until the early ninth century), there is little to disagree with here, and it is only necessary to add a few notes.

The drawing itself is in the round format beloved of the original draughtsman, Beranger, and of others in the dilettante circle of Colonel William Burton (later Conyngham), Beranger's wealthy patron, who lived just down the road in Slane Castle. There is an original Beranger drawing of the subject, but in a rectangular format, preserved in the Royal Irish Academy's manuscript 30.C.30 (p.3), which has a cow in the foreground!

Today the conical cap of the tower is complete, having been restored, along with parts of the top window. Lennox Barrow's book *The Round Towers of Ireland* (1979) gives the text of an inscription on a tablet on the inside wall opposite the doorway, which records the restoration work:

> This tower
> was repaired and restored to its
> original form A.D. 1841 by
> Thomas Rothwell Esq of Blackcastle
> to whom the Blackcastle property
> was left by his second cousin
> Richard Ruxton Fitzherbert

The church ruins beside the tower have, in sad contrast, deteriorated badly since the eighteenth century – the tall gable with belfry on top is now less complete, and the low wall of the church to the right of it has disappeared.

The area around both monuments is now burial ground – although there is only one upright headstone in the drawing, the other stones on the ground looking more like boulder debris left behind by an Ice Age glacier than any grave-markers for the dead. Part of the foreground has now been enclosed by a wall, outside which are trees that obscure the viewpoint used by artist more than 220 years ago.

Church & Tower of Donoghmore *Co. Meath*

DOOR OF THE ROUND TOWER AT DONAGHMORE, CO. MEATH

Here again it was the Huguenot artist Gabriel Beranger who made the original drawing that Cooper has copied. The subject is the same Round Tower seen on the previous page, but this time seen from the other – eastern – side and concentrating just on one important detail, namely the doorway.

Round Tower builders were sparse with their ornamentation and, as Brian Lalor's book *The Irish Round Tower* (1999) points out, the only other example with a sculpted Crucifixion over the doorway is the twelfth-century tower at Brechin in Scotland. But the sculpture on the Donaghmore Round Tower is not without interpretative difficulties.

That the sculpture represents the Crucifixion is not in doubt. The body, head and outstretched arms of Christ are carved on one long, rectangular stone, in a rather rough high relief which may never have had the finer details (for example, hands) sculpted at all. But, beneath it, is the keystone of the arch, on which Christ's lower torso and legs stand out in a lower relief, with the edge of the stone decorated with a simple roll moulding – and this is where we encounter our first problem.

Christ's legs are not straight; rather, the knees are pointing markedly to the right as we look at it, a trait which looks suspiciously late medieval (that is, after 1200), as does the intimation that the feet may be placed one over the other. The sculptural styles of the two stones forming the body of Christ do not fit happily together and, though the roll moulding corresponds to that of the twelfth-century Romanesque canon, one cannot avoid the sneaking suspicion that it could somehow be a later addition.

Adding further to these doubts are the two heads standing out in high relief on the fourth jamb-stone on each side. Beranger/Cooper show both of them as bearded which, if correct, is shown in an exaggerated manner. Neither of the heads looks particularly Romanesque in style, which is what we would expect if the carving were to be dated to the twelfth century, when a number of Irish Round Towers were built. Once again, these have – in my view – the feel of the later medieval period about them, giving rise to the suggestion that most, if not all, of the sculpture on this doorway may be part of a secondary re-modelling carried out a century or more after the tower was originally built.

G. Beranger delin.t.

Ac. fecit. 18 Oct. 1794

Door of the Tower at

Donoghmore — Co.y Meath

BECTIVE ABBEY, Co. MEATH

ooking at Beranger's drawing as copied by Cooper in 1794, one would get the impression that Bective, Co. Meath, must be a castle of some sort – the whole building bristles with towers, and there is hardly anything abbatial about it. However, medieval appearances can be deceptive, and, in reality, Bective is the only Cistercian abbey in the rich county of Meath.

It was a King of Meath – Murchad O'Melaghlin, in fact – who founded Bective as a daughter house of Mellifont in 1147, and its first century of life provided plenty of notoriety. After the Norman baron, Hugh de Lacy, was decapitated in 1186, his body was brought to Bective for burial, while his head went to the Augustinian abbey of St Thomas in Dublin. After years of squabbling between the two institutions as to who should have the re-united parts, the Bishop of Meath, Simon de Rochfort (see no.84), decided that the body should go to the head in Dublin, much to Bective's disgruntlement.

In another incident, in 1217, Bective's abbot became involved in a riot in another Cistercian foundation at Jerpoint, and was later charged with imprisoning a man in a tree-stump until he died – for which crime he was sent to the great French Cistercian house of Clairvaux to be tried.

By 1228, Bective was truly a 'strongly fortified place to which visitors could come in security', in the words of Aubrey Gwynn and RN Hadcock, authors of *Medieval Religious Houses, Ireland* (1970). That tradition seems to have continued into the fifteenth century, when most of the south range of the domestic quarter was built – shown in sunlight in the accompanying drawing. The only parts of the building that date back to the original foundation of the monastery are shown here in shadow – the masonry has one blocked-up arch and another half broken away. These arches belonged to the chapter room, which was part of the complex of buildings on the eastern side of the cloister garth, with its attractive and carved cloister arcade.

The original abbey church lay beyond that wall; what remains of it is not visible on the drawing opposite.

G. Beranger delin.t

A.C. pinx.t 19 Oct. 1794

Abbey of Bective *Co.ᵒ Meath*

ATHLUMNEY CASTLE, Co. MEATH

Immediately approaching Navan, the River Boyne makes a bold sweep around the foot of the hill from which rise up the ruins of Athlumney Castle, built in the style of the end of the 16th century. This pile consists of a large square keep, with stone arched floors and passages rising into a tower from which is a noble view on a clear day. Of the history of this castle, there is little known with certainty. However, its last Lord, Sir Launcelot Dowdall, on hearing the issue of the Battle of the Boyne, and fearing the approach of King William's victorious army, set fire to the castle at nightfall and, crossing the Boyne, sat down upon its opposite bank, from where, as tradition reports, he beheld the last timber in his noble mansion crash amidst the smouldering ruins. All that remains of this castle and estate was forfeited in 1700.

This commentary, probably by Austin Cooper's grandson, Austin Damer Cooper, is written on the page facing the picture of Athlumney Castle, which Cooper copied from a Beranger original of the late 1770s. The brief account is largely taken from *The Beauties of the Boyne and its Tributary, the Blackwater* (second edition, 1850) by William Wilde, polymath and father of Oscar.

William Wilde (later Sir William) gives another interesting footnote about the castle – although, he cautions, it is by no means as likely as the story related above – which refers to a period some forty years earlier. It is said that two sisters occupied the two ancient castles of Athlumney and Blackcastle. The latter was situated on the opposite bank of the river to Athlumney, and its mistress, jealous of her rival on the other side of the river, devised a means of being revenged. She persuaded her sister to enter into an agreement whereby, to prevent their mansions falling into Cromwell's hands, they should each set fire to their own as soon as the news of his approach reached them. A fire lighted upon one was to be the signal for the immediate conflagration of the other. In the meantime, the wily mistress of Blackcastle placed a quantity of dry brushwood on one of the towers of her castle. One night, she lit the brushwood. The inhabitants of Athlumney, perceiving the appointed signal, set fire to their mansion, and burned it to the ground. In the morning, the deception was manifest: Athlumney was a mass of blackened, smoking ruins, while Blackcastle still reared its proud form above the woods, continuing to afford shelter to its haughty mistress.

The castle, as it stands, shows evidence of three separate building periods. The oldest part is the tall tower seen in outline on the left, with a window high in the gable, and turrets at each corner. To the right of it is the manor house, which was added on about 1600. From one side it looks somewhat austere but, from the other side, it is shown to be a grand mansion with mullioned windows surviving in the first and second floors, and an oriel window looking out towards the river. This was probably the building that Sir Launcelot Dowdall saw going up in flames in the 1690s. The third stage of building is represented by the structure in the foreground, which was added after the fire. In the drawing, it looks like the 'tradesman's entrance'. The foreground of the picture is now the green of a modern housing estate.

Castle of Athlumney — Co: Meath

CLONARD CHURCH, Co. MEATH

Clonard is one of the great almost-forgotten monasteries of ancient Ireland. It was here that St Finnian founded his school, which so many of the great sixth-century monastic founders attended – Ciarán of Clonmacnoise, St Colmcille (or Columba) and Brendan the Navigator – making it truly a 'nursery of saints' and marking Finnian out as a very talented and charismatic teacher.

Yet, the sad thing is that not a stone seems to remain upon a stone of this remarkable cradle of Irish monasticism – no sign of an ancient church or cross, let alone a Round Tower, though all of these probably once existed on the site. Even in Cooper's time, any visible ancient remains at Clonard were probably no earlier than Norman, and even since then a number of items have disappeared.

One such disappearance is the church shown in Cooper's copy of Thos. Ashworth's drawing opposite, which looks more like a fortification than a place of prayer. But the lower window splaying outward, and the bell-cote on top, indicate that this was indeed a church, and the cusped window with coat-of-arms on the spandrels almost certainly belonged to it.

In her book, *Clonard, The Story of an Early Irish Monastery 520–1202* (1998), Elizabeth Hickey suggests that this church was part of the ruins of the Augustinian abbey on the site, which had been roofed for divine service and provided with a chimney probably for domestic use. It certainly has nothing to do with the present church, which was built in 1808 and which, sadly, is now itself in a state of ruin. The only item surviving is the charming baptismal font which, in the 1990s, was moved to a position behind the altar of the Catholic church in the village. The font has been described in detail in Helen Roe's charming booklet *The Medieval Fonts of Meath* (1968).

What we see in the drawings are a number of figures in the panels beneath the rim – the second figure from the left is St Peter, holding a scarcely visible key. Then, further to the right comes what appears to be a bishop with staff, an angel holding a book and, on the extreme right, a depiction of the Holy Family's Flight into Egypt. Around the other side is a carving of the Baptism of Christ. Beneath the Flight into Egypt is an angel holding a coat of arms. Dating from around 1500, this font is a late medieval echo of what was once one of the most flourishing monasteries of early medieval Ireland.

Window

Baptismal Font
ae pinxit.

Thos Ashworth delin.   Ale pinxt 23 Oct. 1794

Church of Clonard — Co. Meath

TICROGHAN CASTLE, Co. MEATH

Of all the monuments drawn or, in this instance, copied, by Cooper that have since disappeared, one of the saddest losses must surely be this castle of Ticroghan, only a few miles south-west of Clonard.

Ticroghan was once an imposing cluster of buildings with, on the left, a large three- or four-storey tower house with an almost Romanesque-style doorway, together with another doorway in the end-wall just around the corner. The extravagance of having two entrance doorways can be explained by the probability that there was a protective wall enclosing the tower, which is here represented by just three disconnected fragments with small windows.

On the right is a second tower with equally square-shaped windows, but more slender. It has a conical roof that was still in position when Thos. Ashworth drew the original sketch around 1780. However, when we visit the site today, all we see are earthworks spread over a sizeable field. Some of these may hide the foundations of a major fortification beneath – the outline of a star-shaped fort can easily be traced on the ground. In the background, a cross on a gable seems to mark the presence of a church; however, this may possibly represent the small church that lies a few hundred yards beyond the castle, outside the fortifications.

The castle is also known by the name of Queen Mary's Castle, suggesting that it may have been built in the mid-sixteenth century in the reign of Mary Tudor (Mary I). Its builders may have been the noble FitzGerald family, and it certainly belonged to Sir Luke FitzGerald in 1649 when the earl of Ormonde retired to the castle from Trim, shortly before Cromwell's bloody storming of the walls of Drogheda.

The garrison was under the command of one Sir Robert Talbot, a kinsman of the FitzGeralds, when it was besieged by Cromwellian soldiers, under a man named Commander Reynolds. Relief was expected from Lord Castlehaven, but when it failed to materialise, the garrison surrendered on honourable terms, and the Cromwellians possessed the castle for almost a year. In Sir William Wilde's slightly more colourful version of the story, the Cromwellian besiegers were just about to give up when they noticed that the garrison were firing bullets of silver. Realising they must be in desperate straits to do so, the besiegers persevered with the attack and soon took the fortress.

Tho.ᵗ Ashworth del.ᵗ   J.C. pinᵗ 25.ᵗ Octᵗ 1794

Castle of Tecroghan Co. Meath

CARRICK CASTLE, Co. MEATH

The drawing of Carrick Castle, which Cooper copied in 1794, was probably made by Beranger around 1779, while he was a guest of his patron, Colonel William Burton (later Conyngham), at Slane Castle. Both Carrick and Slane border the north bank of the River Boyne. Carrick, standing about a mile upstream from Slane Castle, forms part of its demesne, as indicated by the townland name – Slane Castle Demesne.

Like Athlumney (no.125), Carrick is a fifteenth- and sixteenth-century tower house with small windows, seen on the left, to which a four-storey manor house was added sometime around 1600. Both parts are very much covered in ivy, and few details such as windows are visible, though a good fireplace is still preserved inside.

Sir William Wilde, in his *Boyne and Blackwater* (1849), relates a local tradition that the castle was erected by the Flemings – the first Norman lords of Slane – as their original residence. However, the castle's old name, Castle Dexter, suggested to Wilde that it was more likely to have been built by the D'Exeter family, whose name was inscribed on a cross erected at Nevinstown near Navan in 1588.

Beneath the castle, the waters of the river cascade gently over a weir. It is said that, in medieval times, any fish caught in the net there caused a bell to ring in the castle's kitchen above, giving the cook notice of what could be served up fresh for dinner.

Castle of Carrick, Co. Meath

DUNMOE CASTLE, Co. MEATH

There were two sibling landscape painters in late eighteenth-century Ireland named Thomas Roberts. The elder died at the age of thirty in 1778, and it was only then that the younger brother, better known as Thomas Sautelle Roberts, took up painting in earnest. He became interested in the Antiquarian movement, and it was probably around 1779 while staying with its prime mover, Colonel William Burton (later Conyngham), at Slane Castle that he painted Dunmoe or Dunmow Castle, which lies only four miles upstream from Slane on the same northern bank of the Boyne.

Opposite is Cooper's copy of what was probably a water-colour by Thomas Sautelle Roberts. Beranger's copy of the same Robert's drawing – probably made within a year or two of the original, and reproduced in my *Beranger's Antique Buildings of Ireland* (1998) – shows how colourful it was, and adds a man and a woman and their dog in the foreground.

The castle itself, possibly dating from the fifteenth century, is a cross between a hall castle and a tower house, having a typically Irish ground plan consisting of a rectangle with rounded bastions at each corner. The tower that we see on the extreme left – that is, on the north-western corner – has totally fallen away, as has the whole back part of the castle. This just leaves the front façade that we see here, facing southwards towards the Boyne, where the water rustles soothingly over a weir.

In 1641, during the Confederate Wars, the castle was taken by ruse, when a forged document was produced that persuaded the garrison to surrender. In the nineteenth century, the cannon ball that Cromwell is said to have fired at the castle on his way to Drogheda in 1649 was used as a weight for a crane.

Sir William Wilde in his invaluable *Boyne and Blackwater* (1849) said that the castle was inhabited during the Williamite Wars and was burned in 1799. That it may have been actually lived in up until or shortly before that date is supported by what looks like a Georgian window, with broken glass, in what was probably the main living room on the first floor.

Castle of Dunmow *Co.* Meath

SLANE ABBEY, Co. MEATH

As well as the artists Gabriel Beranger and Thomas Sautelle Roberts who stayed at Slane Castle and worked for its owner, Colonel William Burton (later Conyngham), in drawing antiquities in the area, we may also add the name of another well-known landscape painter of the late eighteenth-century. This was Jonathan Fisher, whose picture of Slane Abbey was copied by Cooper, and also by Beranger, as can be seen in the National Library of Ireland's manuscript 1958 TX (p.66).

The view from the hill on which the abbey stands is breathtaking. Sweeping southwards over the gently rolling hills of south Co. Meath, it takes in the Hill of Tara where, according to the traditional story, the pagan King Loegaire lost the fight with St Patrick about the lighting of the Pascal Fire. The remains of a small house-shaped tomb in front of the church – not depicted by the artist – is a rare surviving trace of early medieval religious activity on the site. Dúchas, the Irish Heritage Service, recently removed for safekeeping a fragment of a High Cross that had been built into the wall of the church.

The church itself as seen here is that of the Third Order Franciscan regulars, an Order founded by St Francis to cater for lay folk who wanted to participate in the religious life of his Order without becoming full friars. Rather than being divided into a nave and chancel, the church simply has a nave and side aisle, dominated at the western end by an imposing tower that has more than fifty steps leading to the room with the double-light windows seen in the drawing.

Established by 1512, this abbey was one of the last Franciscan foundations before the Reformation. After that, the jurors set up to decide its fate said that the church, chancel and belfry could be 'thrown down' – which, fortunately, they were not. The Lord of Slane continued to lodge priests and prelates there after the suppression, one of whom was captured and executed in 1584. Behind the church was a secular college – curiously omitted by the artist – which was founded at the same time and by the same philanthropic patron, Christopher Fleming of Slane.

Abbey of Slane ~ Co. Meath

GARRAN CASTLE, Co. LAOIS

The castle of Garran in Co. Laois – the Queen's County of the caption – is sometimes called Garranmaconly, after the townland in which it stands some three miles south-west of Borris-in-Ossory, close to the Tipperary border. Situated on a low hill in an area not blessed with many trees, the castle and its tall chimney stand out starkly against the skyline. But the side shown in the picture fell down around 1863, and only the other side survives. Built on the foundation of a rock bluff, its features are very similar to those visible here – a long side of a rectangular tower, a long chute for the garderobe, or toilet, and a neatly rounded corner machicolation from which to shoot at unwanted intruders. The tall chimney at parapet level funnelled smoke out of the fine fireplaces on the first and second floors. Slightly puzzling is the tall slender fragment of what seems to have been another tower just to the right; what its purpose was and how it fitted into the defences is not easy to understand, as it is no longer there.

The castle was built around the first half of the sixteenth century, possibly by the lords of Upper Ossory. Certainly, one hundred years later it was owned by the FitzPatricks, who forfeited it to the Crown. In the late seventeenth century, it was in the possession of the Vicars family, and today it is owned by a welcoming farmer, who lives beside it with his family. Cooper copied his drawing of the castle from an original by a Mr Seymour. There is little information available on this artist, other than that he was an amateur whose pen and brush also brought him into Co. Kilkenny, where he made drawings of antiquities.

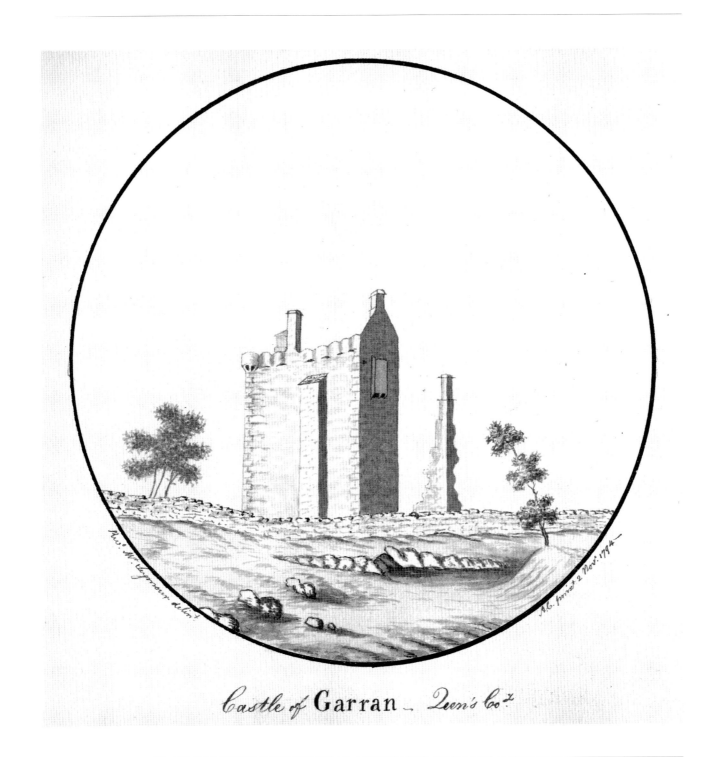

Castle of **Garran** — Queen's Co.

LEA CASTLE, Co. Laois

To the person approaching Lea Castle today, its ivy-covered ruins between the Grand Canal and the River Barrow about two miles east of Portarlington give little idea of how impressive this fortress must have been when Maurice FitzGerald first built it in the thirteenth century. Though it does not seem to be protecting anything of particular strategic significance, its importance may lie in the fact that it was nearly the mid-point of the Province of Leinster.

The centre of the picture is taken up with the tall tower, which had a rounded bastion at each corner, of which only that on the right – with a small cross-shaped arrow-loop near the top – remains intact. The upper part of the tower probably dates from the second half of the thirteenth century.

The low wall that stretches out to the right and left at the foot of the tower is an approximately circular wall that surrounds an earlier motte, upon which the castle was built. Near the left-hand end of this low wall we can see the tall gateway flanked on each side by rounded towers, which gave access to the central tower. But the tall building on the extreme left belongs to a gate-house that allowed traffic to enter an outer open space in front of the tall tower. The tall tower was defended by an outer wall, very low fragments of which can be seen crossing the foreground.

The man whose original drawing Cooper copied here was better known as a patron of architecture than he was as an artist, though his painterly talents were not undistinguished. Cooper gives his name as the Honourable John Dawson. Dawson's original must have been painted before 1786, in which year he was elevated to the peerage and took the title of Lord Carlow. Only four years later Lord Carlow was created earl of Portarlington, whereupon he employed the famous architect James Gandon to build for him a great mansion at Emo, and a church at Coolbanagher nearby.

A similar drawing to the original, though viewing the castle from a slightly different angle, must have been given by Dawson to his friend, the master illustrator Paul Sandby in London. Sandby engraved it with the addition of an enormous tree in the foreground in his *Virtuosi's Museum* of 1779, as reproduced in the 1992 edition of my *Guide to the National and Historic Monuments of Ireland*.

Inside View of Lea *Castle*, Queen's Co.

GLOSSARY

Anta (pl. antae) projecting ends of the long walls of buildings beyond the short gable wall

Ashlar squared, hewn stone

Bartizan defensive structure projecting from the corner of a tower

Bawn area enclosed by a wall adjoining a tower house for the protection of cattle

Bell-cote ornamental structure on a gable top pierced for the hanging of one or more bells

Cicerone a guide

Cinque foils heraldic bearing of a stalk-less flower with five petals

Claustral pertaining to a monastic cloister

Crocket spur- or hook-shaped ornament with flowers or leaves protruding upwards from a canopy or gable

Cusp inward-projecting area or ornament found in Gothic tracery

Cyclopean describing masonry of large irregularly shaped stones

Dexter in heraldry, the side of the shield that is on the *right-hand* side of the wearer but on the spectator's *left*

Donjon tall, often isolated, round tower or bastion

Esker-ridge geological term for a tall worm-like bank meandering along a landscape as a result of glacial activity

Garderobe medieval latrine, privy or lavatory

Garth an enclosure or garden area frequently grassed within a cloister

Impaled heraldic term for the juxtaposition of two escutcheons or shields combined in one

Infula (pl. infulae) a lappet, or flap, hanging from a mitre

Jamb-stone stone forming the side-piece of a doorway

Machicoulis a projecting gallery placed above a door, with holes beneath for pouring boiling substances on unwanted intruders

Martlet heraldic term for a martin or swallow without feet, designating a fourth son

Mendicant a begging friar or pertaining to one of the religious Orders that live by begging

Mullion(ed) upright divisions between the lights of a window

Ogive (ogival) (pertaining to) a pointed arch or window

Oriel a recessed window projecting from a wall and supported by corbels

Portreeve old name for the principal magistrate of a town

Reticulated in the form of a net or network of lines

Sedilia a group of seats in a chancel wall for the use of officiating clergy

Soffit the underside of a doorway, arch or lintel

Spandrel the irregular triangular space between the curve of an arch and the upper corner of its right-angled frame

String-course horizontal line of masonry projecting from the face of a building

Tracery the stone filling of Gothic arched windows

Transom(ed) (pertaining to) the horizontal cross-bar of a window

CONCORDANCES

To offer the reader the correct accession and page numbers of the drawings reproduced in this volume, it is necessary to supply an abbreviated concordance, as follows.

The concordance of the illustrations numbered 1–90 in this book is relatively straightforward. All of these drawings come from the *first* album (accession number 2122 TX (1)). However, the first page of this album is missing. Therefore, no.1 reproduced here is actually p.2 of the album, no.2 reproduced here is p.3 of the album and so on.

The concordance of the illustrations numbered 91–132 in this book is slightly more complex. Because the *second* album (accession number 2122 TX (2)) contains material not in Cooper's hand, it is not reproduced in its entirety in this book. The concordance of nos. 91–132 (which are by Cooper) with that of the appropriate page of the second album is therefore as follows.

SUBJECTS IN 2122 TX (2) BY COOPER

Illo. no.	Subject	Page in album 2122 TX (2)
91	Ardfinnan Castle, Co. Tipperary	1
92	Charles Fort, Co. Cork	2
93	Monasterboice – SE View, Co. Louth	6
94	Monasterboice – NE View, Co. Louth	7
95	Ferns Abbey and Church, Co. Wexford	8
96	Taghmon Castle, Co. Wexford	9
97	Roscrea Abbey, Co. Tipperary	10
98	Carmelite Friary, Kildare	11
99	Grenoge Motte, Co. Westmeath	12
100	Creevelea Abbey, Co. Leitrim	13

SUBJECTS IN 2122 TX (2) NOT BY COOPER

The drawings in Cooper's second album (National Library accession number 2122 TX (2)) that are *not* by Cooper are listed below:

Other Cooper drawings in the National Library of Ireland

In addition to the drawings reproduced here, there are some plans and miscellaneous sketches by Austin Cooper, which now form part of his collection in the National Library, and which are listed here for the sake of completeness. Some however, are unsigned, and can only tentatively be ascribed to Cooper. Most are contained in the album bearing the accession number 2122 TX (4), and have the following page numbers and subjects:

1. Ballintober, Co. Mayo – Door, window and console (after Beranger) – signed AC, dated October 1799
4. Murrisk Abbey, Co. Mayo – Plan – signed AC, dated October 1799
5. St Selsker's Church, Wexford – Plan – unsigned, but probably by Cooper
6. Cong Abbey, Co. Mayo – Plan (after Bigari) – signed AC, dated October 1799
7. Roserk Abbey, Co. Mayo – Window details (after Beranger) – signed AC, dated October 1799
14. Cong Abbey, Co. Mayo – architectural details (after Beranger) – signed AC, dated October 1799
16. Rathcroghan, Co. Roscommon – Plan – (unsigned, but probably Austin Cooper after Beranger)
17. Rath of Ballytrant, Co. Wexford – Plan – signed AC, dated October 1799
19. Ferns, Co. Wexford – Heads of High Crosses (unsigned – Austin Cooper? Undated)
20. O'Rourke's Castle, Co. Leitrim – Plan – and windows of the Abbey of Drumahair, Co. Leitrim signed AC, dated October 1799
24. Ballylaghan Castle, Co. Mayo – Plan (after Beranger) – signed AC, dated October 1799
25. Ferns Cathedral, Co. Wexford – Plan – signed AC, dated October 1799
28. Bridge Castle, Thurles, Co. Tipperary – Plan – signed AC, dated October 1799
31. Cong Abbey, Co. Mayo – Plan (after Bigari) – signed AC, dated April 1800
35. Burrishool Abbey, Co. Mayo – Plan – signed (unusually) A Cooper FSA, undated
37. Clonmacnoise, Co. Offaly – Front door of the Cathedral, with details (after Beranger) – signed AC, dated October 1799.

39. Clonmacnoise, Co. Offaly – Door of the Chapel (St Finghin's) with detail of door and inscription (after Beranger) – signed AC, dated October 1799
40. Clonmacnoise, Co. Offaly – Door and window details – signed AC, dated October 1799

Furthermore, 2122 TX (96) has a plan of Multifernam, Co. Westmeath (after Bigari), signed AC and dated November 1799. The author hopes to publish a number of these in a visual reconstruction of Beranger and Bigari's tour of Connacht in 1779.

In addition to the above, the National Library recently acquired three separate Austin Cooper drawings, as follows:
2122 TX (106) Castle of Holdins-rath, Co. Kilkenny – After Brien – signed AC, dated 28 October 1799
2122 TX (107) Castle and Church of Dungarvan, Co. Kilkenny – After Brien – signed AC, dated 26 October 1799
2122 TX (108) Castle in Ballinchalla Island in Lough Mask, Co. Mayo – After Beranger – signed AC, dated 10 October, 1799

These three items were sold at Messrs Mealy's auction in Dublin in early December 1999, and were published prior to auction by Conleth Manning in an article entitled 'Some unpublished Austin Cooper illustrations', which appeared in *The Journal of Irish Archaeology* Vol. IX, 1998, 127–34.

This article – and the auction – contained four further Cooper drawings:
1. Castle of Bishop's-lough, Co. Kilkenny (after Brien) – signed AC, dated October 1799
2. Castle of Struan, Co. Kilkenny (unsigned and undated, but probably by Cooper)
3. Castle of Glynn, Co. Limerick, Taken from the Inn Window – originally drawn by Cooper 17 July 1796, signed AC, and painted 14 August 1796.
4. Castle of Disart, Co. Kilkenny (after Brien) – signed AC, dated 29 October, 1799

The first two of these are owned by Mr William Murphy, of Castlegarden, Thomastown, Co. Kilkenny. The third is owned by the Knight of Glin. The present location of the last drawing, Disart Castle, has yet to be established.

SELECT BIBLIOGRAPHY OF WORKS CONSULTED

Abbreviations:

JCHAS Journal of the Cork Historical and Archaeological Society

JCLAS Journal of the County Louth Archaeological Society

JGAHS Journal of the Galway Archaeological and Historical Society

JKAS Journal of the (County) Kildare Archaeological Society (and surrounding districts)

JRSAI Journal of the Royal Society of Antiquaries of Ireland (incorporating earlier journals with different titles)

Mem. Dead Ireland Journal of the Society for the Preservation of the Memorials of the Dead, Ireland

PRIA Proceedings of the Royal Irish Academy

Anon 'A visit to Innismurray', *The Protestant Penny Magazine* 1, 1834, no. 5, 65–69 and no. 6, 102–04.

Anon 'History of St Wolstan's', *The Irish Builder*, 1 June and 1 July 1899.

Anon 'Proceedings', *JRSAI* 46, 1916, 202–4 (Duleek).

Anon 'Termonfeckin Castle', *JCLAS* 5, 1921, 58.

Bagwell, Richard *Ireland under the Stuarts and during the Interregnum*, Vol. II (London 1909).

Barrow, George Lennox *The Round Towers of Ireland* (Dublin 1979).

Barberstown Castle (Hotel history), Straffan, n.d.

Bence-Jones, Mark *Burke's Guide to Country Houses*, Vol. I, Ireland (London 1978).

Beranger, Gabriel 'Inishmurray – Letter from Gabriel Beranger to Charles Vallancey, 26 May 1785', *Ireland of the Welcomes* 42 (5), September–October 1993, 30–33.

Berger, Rainer 'Radiocarbon Dating of Early Medieval Irish Monuments', *PRIA* 95 C, 1995, 159–74.

Boylan, Lena 'Kildrought Church and Cemetery, part 3, Of Whistlers and Runners', in *Celbridge Charter* no. 52, August 3rd, 1977.

Boylan, Lena 'The Wonderful Barn', *JKAS* 18(3), 1996–97, 337–47.

Buckley, Victor M and Sweetman, P David *Archaeological Survey of County Louth* (Dublin 1991).

Callery, Philip 'Priory of St John the Baptist, Newtown Trim', *Irish Ecclesiastical Record* 16 (5th ser.), 1929, 105–113.

Callery, Philip 'The Abbey of SS Peter and Paul, Newtown Trim', *Irish Ecclesiastical Record* 16 (5th ser.), 1920, 483–96.

Cane, R Claude 'St Wolstan's Priory, Celbridge', *JRSAI* 49, 1919, 55–59.

Carrigan, William *The History and Antiquities of the Diocese of Ossory*, 4 vols (Dublin 1905).

Carrigan, W, McEnery, MJ and Garstin, JR 'The Neale Park Monument, Kilmolara Parish', *Mem. Dead Ireland* 7 (3,2), 1909, 638–45.

Carroll, FM 'Some Notes on the Abbey and Cross of Moone and other places in the Valley of the Griese', *JKAS* 1 (5), 1894, 286–94.

Casey, Christine and Rowan, Alistair *North Leinster* (London 1993).

Clapham, Alfred 'Some Minor Irish Cathedrals' *The Archaeological Journal* 106, Supplement 1952, 16–39.

Clyne, Miriam 'Interim Report on the Archaeological Excavations at Moone Abbey, Co. Kildare', *JKAS* 18(4), 1998–99, 473–92.

Cochrane, Robert 'Abbey Knockmoy, County Galway, notes on the buildings and "frescoes"', *JRSAI* 34, 1904, 244–53.

Cochrane, Robert 'Notes on the Round Tower &c, of Kilmacduagh', *JRSAI* 34, 1904, 234–38.

Cochrane, Robert 'Notes on the Augustinian Priory of Athassel, County Tipperary', *JRSAI* 39, 1909, 279–89.

Cogan, A *The Diocese of Meath, Ancient and Modern*, Vol. II (Dublin 1867).

Collins, Tracy 'Hore Abbey, Cashel; the Archaeological Record', *Tipperary Historical Journal* 1998, 234–40.

Commins, John 'Notes on the places of antiquarian interest visited by the Society, May 1906', *JRSAI* 36, 1906, 272–75 (Callan).

Cooper, R Austin *Butterhill & Beyond* (Hurst, Reading 1991).

Cox, Liam *Moate, County Westmeath. A History of the Town and District* (Moate 1981).

Craig, Maurice *The Architecture of Ireland from the Earliest Times to 1880* (London 1982).

Craig, Maurice and Craig, Michael *Mausolea Hibernica* (Dublin 1999).

Crawford, Henry S 'The Mural Paintings and Inscriptions at Knockmoy Abbey', *JRSAI* 49, 1919, 25–34.

Crawford, Henry S 'The Round Tower and Castle of Timahoe', *JRSAI* 54, 1924, 31–45.

Creevelea Abbey, Co. Leitrim (official guidebook), Dublin, n.d.

Crookshank, Anne and the Knight of Glin *The Watercolours of Ireland* (London 1994).

Cunningham, George *Roscrea and District* (Roscrea 1976).

Cunningham, George *The Anglo-Norman Advance into the South-West Midlands of Ireland, 1185–1221* (Roscrea 1987).

De Burgh, Thomas J 'Ancient Naas. V. – Topographical', *JKAS* 1 (5), 1894, 318–36.

Deevy, Mary B *Medieval Ring Brooches in Ireland* (Bray 1998).

Dunraven, Caroline Countess of *Memorials of Adare Manor* (Oxford 1865).

Everard, HAJ 'The Family of Everard, Part II', *The Irish Genealogist* 7, 1989, 505–42.

Everard, John 'Everard's Castle, now Burncourt Castle, near Cahir, County Tipperary', *JRSAI* 37, 1907, 74–85.

Fennessy, Ignatius 'The Franciscan Friary of Kildare', *JKAS* 8 (3), 1996–97, 322–36.

FitzGerald, Lord Walter 'The Round Towers of Kildare: their Origin and Use', *JKAS* 1 (2), 1892, 71–94.

FitzGerald, Lord Walter 'Kilkea Castle', *JKAS* 2 (1) 1896, 3–32

FitzGerald, Lord Walter 'Great Connell Abbey, Co. Kildare', *JKAS* 2 (5), 1898, 304–14.

FitzGerald, Lord Walter 'St Peter's Parish – Drogheda', *Mem. Dead Ireland* 4 (2), 1899, 276–79.

FitzGerald, Lord Walter 'New Abbey of Kilcullen', *JKAS* 3 (5), 1901, 301–17.

FitzGerald, Lord Walter 'The History and Antiquities of the Queen's County Barony of Portnahinch, Part II, Morett and Coolbanagher', *JKAS* 4 (2), 1904, 285–311.

FitzGerald, Lord Walter 'Kilconnell Village Cross', *Mem. Dead Ireland* 6, 1904–06, 326–27.

FitzGerald, Lord Walter 'The History and Antiquities of the Queen's County Barony of Portnahinch, Part III, Lea Castle', *JKAS* 4 (5), 1905, 325–51.

FitzGerald, Lord Walter 'The Castle and Manor of Carlow, Part II', *JKAS* 6 (5), 1910, 365–76.

FitzGerald, Lord Walter 'Tyrrell's Mill and Castle, near Celbridge', *JKAS* 6 (6), 1911, 520–22.

Flanagan, Urban G 'Our Lady of Graces of Youghal – III, History of the Image', *JCHAS* 56, 1951, 1–10.

Galway, Fiona 'Meath Tower houses', *Ríocht na Midhe* 7 (4) 1985–86, 28–59.

Gaughan, J Anthony *Listowel and its Vicinity* (Cork 1973).

Georgian Society Records, The, Vol. V, 1913.

Gleeson, Dermot F 'The castle and manor of Nenagh, with a description of the buildings by HG Leask', *JRSAI* 66, 1936, 247–69.

Gleeson, Dermot F *Roscrea* (Dublin 1947).

Gleeson, Dermot F and Gwynn, Aubrey *A History of the Diocese of Killaloe,* Vol. I (Dublin 1962).

Grose, Francis *The Antiquities of Ireland* (ed. Edward Ledwich), 2 vols, London 1791–95.

Gwynn, Aubrey and Hadcock, R Neville *Medieval Religious Houses, Ireland* (London 1970).

Halpin, Andrew and Buckley, Laureen 'Archaeological excavations at the Dominican priory, Drogheda, Co. Louth', *PRIA* 95 C, 1995, 175–253.

Halpin, Eoin 'Excavation at St Mary d'Urso, Drogheda, Co. Louth', *JCLAS* 23 (4), 1996, 452–509.

Harbison, Peter *The High Crosses of Ireland,* 3 vols (Bonn 1992).

Harbison, Peter *Irish High Crosses with the Figure Sculptures Explained* (Drogheda 1994).

Harbison, Peter *The Crucifixion in Irish Art* (Harrisburg, Pa./Dublin 2000)

Harris, Walter 'The Whole Works of Sir James Ware Concerning Ireland, revised and improved', Vol. I *The History of the Bishops of That Kingdom,* Dublin 1764.

Hayman, Canon *Memorials of Youghal, Ecclesiastical and Civil* (Youghal 1879).

Healy, James N *The Castles of County Cork* (Cork/Dublin 1988).

Heraughty, Patrick *Inishmurray, Ancient Monastic Island* (Dublin 1982).

Hickey, Elizabeth *Clonard, the Story of an Early Irish Monastery, 520–1202* (Leixlip 1998).

Hodkinson, Brian J 'Excavations in the gatehouse of Nenagh Castle, 1996 and 1997', *Tipperary Historical Journal* 1999, 162–82.

Hore, Philip Herbert *History of the Town and County of Wexford,* London, V (1906) and VI (1911).

Hunt, John *Irish Medieval Figure Sculpture,* 2 vols (Dublin/London 1974).

Jordan, AJ 'Date, chronology and evolution of the County Wexford tower house', *Journal of the Wexford Historical Society* 13, 1990–91, 30–81.

Kelly, Martin J 'The owners and tenants of Barberstown castle', *JKAS* 16 (1), 1977–78, 61–67.

Kelly, Richard J 'The name and family of Ouseley', *JRSAI* 40, 1910, 132–46.

Kenney, James F *The Sources for the Early History of Ireland: Ecclesiastical* (New York 1929).

Kerrigan, Paul 'Charles Fort, Kinsale', *The Irish Sword* 13 (no. 53), 1978–79, 323–28.

Kerrigan, Paul *Castles and Fortifications in Ireland 1485–1945* (Cork 1995).

Keys, Brian and Landers, Sean *Old Kilcullen, A Guide to its History and Antiquities* (Kilcullen 1978).

Killanin, Lord and Duignan, Michael V *The Shell Guide to Ireland,* 2nd ed. (London 1967).

King, Heather A 'Late medieval crosses in County Meath, c.1470–1635', *PRIA* 84 C, 1984, 79–115.

King, Heather A 'Irish wayside and churchyard crosses 1600–1700', *Post-Medieval Archaeology* 19, 1985, 13–33.

King, Heather A 'The medieval and seventeenth-century carved stone collection in Kildare', *JKAS* 17, 1987–91, 59–95.

King, Heather A, Grogan, Eoin and Bradley, John 'Archaeological excavations in the environs of a motte and bailey at Ballinaclogh Lower, near Timahoe, Co. Laois', *JKAS* 18 (3), 1996–97, 322–36.

Kirkpatrick, WT 'St Wolstan's', *JKAS* 2 (5) 1898, 283–88.

Lageniensis 'Old Churches of Leix, no. LXXVII – Durrow or Castle Durrow', *The Irish Builder,* July 15, 1887, 200.

Lalor, Brian *The Irish Round Tower* (Cork 1999).

Leask, HG 'Bective Abbey, Co. Meath', *JRSAI* 46, 1916, 46–57.

Leask, HG *Fore, Co. Westmeath* (official guide), Dublin c.1939.

Leask, HG 'Mallow Castle, Co. Cork', *JCHAS* 49, 1944, 19–24.

Leask, HG *Early Irish Churches and Monastic Buildings,* 3 Vols (Dublin 1955–60).

Leask, HG *Irish Castles and Castellated Houses* (Dundalk 1964).

Mac an Bháird Michael 'Mornington or Marinerstown', *Dinnseanchas* 3 (3), 1969, 73–75.

Marnane, Denis G 'Samuel Cooper of Killenure (1750–1831) – A Tipperary Land Agent and His Diaries', *Tipperary Historical Journal* 1993, 102–27.

McConnell, Sean 'Work on Abbey's Mural Almost Completed', *The Irish Times,* September 6, 1989.

McDonnell-Garvey, Maire 'Banada Abbey, a short history', *The Corran Herald* 32, 1999/2000, 9–11.

McNeill, Tom *Castles in Ireland, Feudal Power in a Gaelic World* (London/New York 1997).

McParland, Edward *Thomas Ivory, Architect*, Gatherum series 4 (Ballycotton 1973).

Metternich, Wolfgang *Burgen in Irland, Herrschaftsarchitektur im Hochmittelalter* (Darmstadt 1999).

Mitchell, J 'Mayor Lynch of Galway, a review of the tradition', *JGAHS* 32, 1966–71, 5–72.

Moloney, Michael 'Mungret', *North Munster Antiquarian Journal* 4 (1), 1944, 1–15.

Moore, Michael J *Archaeological Inventory of County Meath* (Dublin 1987).

Murphy, Denis 'Kildare: its history and antiquities', *JKAS* 2 (5), 1898, 289–302

Murphy, Donal 'Archaeological excavations at the Magdalene Tower, Drogheda, Co. Louth', *JCLAS* 24 (1), 1997, 75–128.

Murtagh, Ben 'The Castles of Naas', *JKAS* 16 (4), 1983/84, 355–61.

Murtagh, Harman 'The Town Wall Fortifications of Athlone, in H Murtagh (ed.)', *Irish Midland Studies, Essays in Commemoration of N.W. English*, 89–106 (Athlone 1980).

Murtagh, Harman 'Athlone', *Irish Historic Towns Atlas* 6 (Dublin 1994).

Neary, J 'On the history and antiquities of the parish of Dunmore', *JGAHS* 8, (1913–14), 94–128.

O'Brien, Jacqueline and Harbison, Peter *Ancient Ireland* (London 1996).

O'Conor, Kieran 'The Origins of Carlow Castle', *Archaeology Ireland* 11 (3), 1997, 13–16.

O hIceadha, G 'Excavation of church site in Old Kilcullen townland, Co. Kildare', *JRSAI* 61, 1941, 148–51.

O'Keeffe, Peter and Simington, Tom *Irish Stone Bridges, History and Heritage* (Dublin 1991).

O'Keeffe, Tadhg *An Anglo-Norman Monastery. Bridgetown Priory and the Architecture of the Augustinian Canons Regular in Ireland* (Cork/Kinsale 1999).

O'Kelly, MJ 'Some prehistoric monuments of Imokilly', *JCHAS* 50, 1945, 10–23.

Ó Nualláin, Séan and Cody, Eamon 'A re-examination of four sites in Grange townland, Lough Gur, County Limerick', *North Munster Antiquarian Journal* 37, 1996, 3–14.

Parliamentary Gazetteer of Ireland, The. 3 vols (Dublin/London/Edinburgh 1846).

P(etrie, George) 'Ardfinnan Castle, County of Tipperary', *The Irish Penny Journal* 1 (no. 44), May 1, 1841, 345–46.

Power, Denis et al *Archaeological Inventory of County Cork*, Vol. 2, East and South Cork (Dublin 1994).

Price, Liam (ed.) *An Eighteenth Century Antiquary, The sketches, Notes and Diaries of Austin Cooper (1759–1830)*, Dublin 1942.

Raymond, P 'The Condons of Cloghleigh, Barony of Condons and Clongibbons', *JCHAS* Series ll, 2, 1896, 477–85 and 509–15.

Roe, Helen *Medieval Fonts of Meath* (n.p., 1968).

Roe, Helen 'Cadaver effigial monuments in Ireland', *JRSAI* 99, 1969, 1–19.

Roe, Helen *Monasterboice and its Monuments* (n.p., 1981).

Salter, Mike *Castles and Stronghouses of Ireland* (Malvern 1993).

Spellissy, Seán *The History of Limerick City* (Limerick 1998).

Stalley, Roger *The Cistercian Monasteries of Ireland* (London/New Haven 1987).

Stalley, Roger 'The Anglo-Norman keep at Trim: its archaeological implications', *Archaeology Ireland* 6 (4), 1992, 16–19.

Stokes, Margaret 'Old Kilcullen', *JKAS* 2 (7), 1899, 431–46.

Story, George *An Impartial History of the Wars in Ireland* (London 1693).

Stout, Geraldine 'Trial excavations at Roscrea castle, County Tipperary', *Éile. The Journal of the Roscrea Heritage Society* 2, 1983–84, 29–42.

Stout, Geraldine *Archaeological Survey of the Barony of Ikerrin* (Roscrea 1984),

Strickland, WG 'Carved stone from Monksgrange, Queen's Co.', *JRSAI* 52, 1922, 82–83.

Sweetman, David *The Medieval Castles of Ireland* (Cork 1999).

Sweetman, David, Alcock, Olive and Moran, Bernie *Archaeological Inventory of County Laois* (Dublin 1995).

Tallon, Maura 'An Irish medieval manuscript in Hereford Cathedral', *An Leabharlann* 21, (2), June 1963, 63–67.

Tuite, James 'Historic ruins in Westmeath', *JRSAI*, 40, 1910, 354–55.

Ua Bradaigh, Tomás 'Miscellanea (Bellewstown)', *Ríocht na Midhe* 2 (4), 1962, 67–69.

Vigors, Colonel 'Report (Leighlinbridge)', *JRSAI* 18, 1887–88, 479.

Wakeman, WF *A Survey of the Antiquarian Remains on the Island of Inishmurray* (London/Edinburgh 1893).

Walker, JC *An Historical Essay on the Dress of the Ancient and Modern Irish* (London 1788).

Westropp, Thomas Johnson 'Killaloe: its Ancient Palaces and Cathedral (Part II)', *JRSAI* 23, 1893, 187–201.

Westropp, Thomas Johnson 'Ennis Abbey and the O'Brien tombs', *JRSAI* 25, 1895, 135–54 and 231.

Westropp, Thomas Johnson '"Slane in Bregia," County Meath: its friary and hermitage', *JRSAI* 31, 1901, 405–24 and 32, 1902, 192.

Westropp, Thomas Johnson 'The Ancient Castles of County Limerick', *PRIA* 26 C, 1906–07, 55–108 and 143–264.

Westropp, Thomas Johnson, Macalister, RAS and Macnamara, GU *The Antiquities of Limerick and its Neighbourhood*, Royal Society of Antiquaries of Ireland, Antiquarian handbook series VII (Dublin 1916).

Wilde, William R *The Beauties of the Boyne, and its Tributary, the Blackwater*, 2nd ed. (Dublin 1850).

Wilde, William R *A Memoir of Gabriel Beranger and his Labours in the Cause of Irish Art and Antiquities from 1760 to 1780* (Dublin 1880).

Wright, Thomas *Louthiana* (London 1748).

These maps are designed to give the approximate locations of the monuments illustrated in this volume, county by county. Because of a concentration of sites within the 80-mile radius of Dublin, most of Leinster is given in enlarged format on p.287. The numbers on the maps refer to the monuments listed in the text (nos. 1–132) and not to their page numbers.

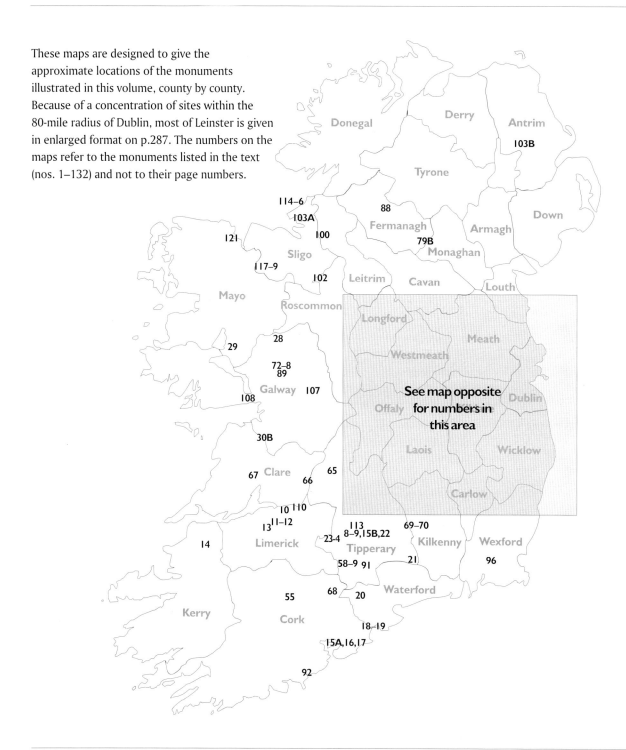

Donegal

Derry

Antrim

103B

Tyrone

Down

114–6

103A

88

Armagh

121

Fermanagh

79B

Monaghan

100

Sligo

117–9

102

Leitrim

Cavan

Louth

Mayo

Roscommon

Longford

Meath

28

Westmeath

29

72–8

89

Galway

107

See map opposite for numbers in this area

Offaly

Dublin

108

30B

Laois

Wicklow

67

Clare

65

66

Carlow

10 110

13 11–12

113

8–9,15B,22

69–70

14

Limerick

23-4

Tipperary

Kilkenny

Wexford

58–9 91

21

96

55

68

20

Waterford

Kerry

Cork

18–19

15A,16,17

92

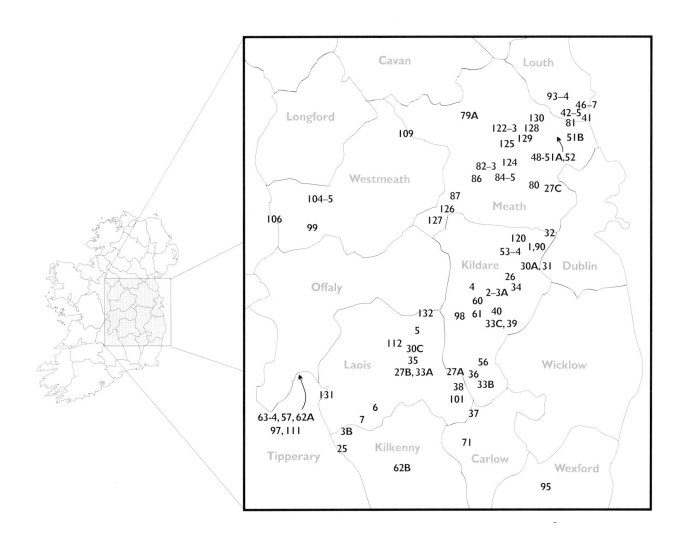

INDEX

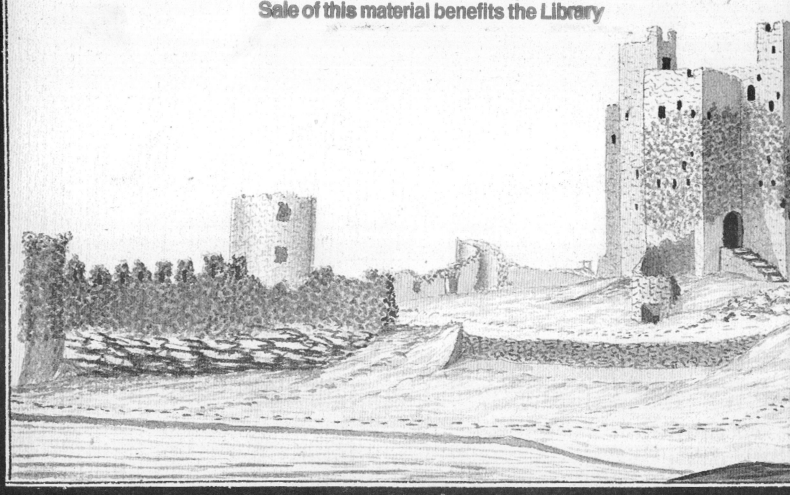

Ple: delurt: 15.ᵗ May 1785

A N: View of the Castle of Tri